IMO OLYMPIAD WORKBOOK

5

SOF INTERNATIONAL MATHEMATICS OLYMPIAD 2023-24

SANAGE EDITORIAL BOARD

SANAGE

PUBLISHING HOUSE

Paperback: 978-811937380-2

Printed by:

Sanage Publishing House LLP
Mumbai, India

sanagepublishing@gmail.com

Contents

NUMBER SENSE

TOPICS COVERED:

* Numerals and number names
* Place value and face value in the indian and international system of numeration
* Roman Numbers
* Estimation to nearest ten's, hundred's and thousand's
* Formation of a number using given information
* Expanded form
* Ascending and descending order
* Word problems

MATHEMATICAL REASONING

1. **What is the numeral form of the number name given below?**

   'Two hundred three thousand, five hundred twenty three'

   A) 23,53   B) 23,523   C) 203,523   D) 203,522

2. **The sum of place values of all the digits of the number 528914 is ___.**

   A) 94   B) 500000   C) 29   D) 528914

3. **Roman numeral for the greatest four-digit number is___.**

   A) CMIXIX   B) IXCMXCIX   C) $\overline{IX}$IXIXIX   D) CMIIC

4. **Four million four thousand forty is same as____.**

   A) 4040040   B) 40040040   C) 4040400   D) 909090

5. **In 768162, the place value of 6 at ten thousand places is ___ times the place value of 6 at tens place.**

   A) 10   B) 1000   C) 100   D) 10000

6.   **Which of the following Roman numerals is meaningless?**

A) XL   B) XC   C) LT   D) LX

7.   **Seven lakh twenty two thousand four hundred seventeen can be written in international system of numeration as ___.**

A) 722,417   B) 7,022,417   C) 7,022,417   D) 72,2,41,477

8.   **Compare and fill in the box.**

$$DCCC \boxed{} LXXX$$

A) >   B) =   C) <   D) Can't be determined

9.   **Roman numeral for 115 is ___.**

A) CIX   B) CXV   C) CVII   D) LIX

10.   **What will we get, if we add 1 to the largest 4-digit number?**

A) 10000   B) 19999   C) 99999   D) 10009

11.   **10 Lakh=___.**

A) 1 million   B) 10 million   C) 100 million   D) 10 crores

12.   **Which of the following options is the successor of the number 424520?**

A) 424519   B) 424521   C) 424522   D) 424520

13.   **Round off the number 92891 to nearest hundreds.**

A) 92900   B) 92800   C) 92890   D) 90000

14.   **The difference between the place values of the encircled digits of the given number is ___.**

42, 3, ⑤, 2,160, and 24, 6, ⑧, 962

A) 42000   B) 45000   C) 8000   D) 55000

15.   **Predecessor of smallest 5-digit number is ____.**

A) Ten thousand   B) One thousand one hundred eleven

C) One lakh   D) Nine thousand nine hundred ninety nine

16. **Which of the following options is arranged is ascending order?**

    A) 4,52,790 : 4,52,785 : 4,45,990 : 4,30,330

    B) 9,22,320 : 9,23,420 : 9,23,878 : 9,24,520

    C) 1,02,520 : 1,21,590 : 1,00,001 : 1,22,230

    D) 8,23,00 : 8,23,220 : 8,23,880 : 8,23,111

17. **Face value of 5 in 3,11,528 is ___.**

    A) Five   B) Five hundred   C) Fifty two   D) Fifty

18. **Which of the following will be greatest, if each number is rounded off to nearest thousands?**

    A) 4,85,932   B) 4,80,508   C) 4,86,702   D) 4,85,320

19. **Select the INCORRECT match.**

    A) 80000 + 3000 +100+40 +9 =83149

    B) 900000 +20000 +700 +60 +8 =920768

    C) 100000 +80000 +500 +40 +8 =18548

    D) 30000 +3000 +400 +50 +5 =33455

20. **Smallest 4 digit number that can be formed by using digits 5,3,1 and 7 each at least once is___.**

    A) 7531   B) 5713   C) 3157   D) 1357

EVERYDAY MATHEMATICS

21. **The height of pole P is DXXX cm and the height of pole Q is DL cm. Who is shortest among them?**

    A) Pole P   B) Pole Q

C) Both have same heights   D) Can't be determined

22. **Anil spent DCLXV amount in the market. What is the Hindu-Arabic number for this Roman number?**

    A) 990   B) 550   C) 665   D) 1000

23. **Saket has five cards having digits 3,4,2,1,5 and 6. The smallest 6-digit even number that Saket can form using these digits each only once is ___.**

    A) 654321   B) 132456   C) 432156   D) 123456

24. **Rupa makes a profit of rupees fifty two crore twelve lakh sixty six thousand twenty two, Her profit can be written in Indian system as**

    A) Rs. 523,66,222   B) Rs. 52,12,66,022

    C) Rs. 52,12,66,220   D) Rs. 5,212,66

25. **Auditorium A has 637441 seats, auditorium B has 637544 seats, auditorium C has 647941 seats and auditorium D has 629870 seats. which auditorium has the most number of seats?**

    A) Auditorium B   B) Auditorium D
    C) Auditorium C   D) Auditorium A

ACHIEVERS SECTION (HOTS)

26. **Three girls Jyoti, Swapna and Akshya wrote 3 different numbers and makes the following statement.**

    Jyoti : My number is MCLXX.

    Swapna : My number is the successor of jyoti's number.

    Akshaya : My number is the predecessor of jyoti's number.

    What numbers are thought by Swapna and Akshaya respectively?

A) 1171, 1169   B) 1559, 1560   C) 1011, 1001   D) 1560, 1561

27. Which of the following statements is CORRECT?

A) The place value of the digit '9' in the number 468913 is 90.

B) In the number 6590324. The place value of the digit '6' is 6000000.

C) The place value of the digit '7' in the number 765490 is predecessor of 765499.

D) The place value of the digit '5' in the number 245700 is successor of 40000.

28. Mukta is thinking of a 5-digit number. The unit's place digit is an odd prime number. The ten's place digit is the predecessor of thousand's place digit. The hundred's place digit is the smallest odd number. The ten thousand's place digit is an even prime number. There are only 2 even digits in the number. What could be the number Mukta is thinking of?

A) 23180   B) 23183   C) 29182   D) 29185

29. Select the INCORRECT option.

A) 1350 – MCCLL   B) 1400 – MCD

C) 1051-MLI   D) 1100 – MC

30. Match the columns.

Column 1	Column 2
(P) Eighty four lakh seventy one thousand four hundred seventy one	(1) 32,42,499
(Q) Thirty two lakh fourty two thousand four hundred ninety nine.	(2) 14,21,498
(R) Fourteen lakh twenty one thousand four hundred ninety eight.	(3) 79,48,880
(S) Seventy nine lakh fourty eight	(4) 84,71,471

thousand eight hundred eighty

	(P)	(Q)	(R)	(S)
A)	4	2	1	3
B)	4	1	2	3
C)	3	1	4	2
D)	1	3	2	4

Colour your choice with color pencil

1	2	3	4	5
A B C D	A B C D	A B C D	A B C D	A B C D
6	**7**	**8**	**9**	**10**
A B C D	A B C D	A B C D	A B C D	A B C D
11	**12**	**13**	**14**	**15**
A B C D	A B C D	A B C D	A B C D	A B C D
16	**17**	**18**	**19**	**20**
A B C D	A B C D	A B C D	A B C D	A B C D
21	**22**	**23**	**24**	**25**
A B C D	A B C D	A B C D	A B C D	A B C D
26	**27**	**28**	**29**	**30**
A B C D	A B C D	A B C D	A B C D	A B C D

CHAPTER 2

COMPUTATION OPERATIONS

TOPICS COVERED:

* Addition, subtraction, multiplication and division
* Estimated sum, difference, multiplication and division by rounding off
* Sum, difference, multiplication and division of Roman numbers
* Properties of sum, difference, product and division
* Factor and multiples, common factors and multiples
* Hightest Common Factor (H.C.F) and Least Common Multiple (L.C.M)
* Prime factors of numbers
* Complex word problems, unitary method to solve problems

MATHEMATICAL REASONING

1. **Find the value of CMXXIX+CMXII**

    A) CMMXII   B) MDCMXII   C) CMXIICCM   D) MDCCCXLI

2. **Fathom is a unit used by sailors to measure the depth of water. If a submarine is located underwater at 240 feet, then which expression would describe the location of the submarine in fathoms?**

    | 1 Fathom = 6 feet |

    A) 240 × 6   B) 240 ÷ 6   C) 240 + 6   D) 240 - 6

3. **Study the following statements and select the correct option.**

    Statement 1: Symbol L can be subtracted from V and X only once.

    Statement 2: Symbol X can be subtracted from L

    A) Both statement-1 and statement-2 are true

B) Statement -1 is false, but statement-2 is true.

C) Statement-1 is true, but statement-2 is false.

D) Both statement-1 and statement-2 are false.

4. Which of the following number is not a prime?

A) 71   B) 79   C) 45   D) 37

5. Which of the following options makes the given expression true?

$$\textbf{DCLXX-CDLV} \boxed{} \textbf{CCLX+LXXX}$$

A) <   B) >   C) +   D) Can't be determined

6. A factory produced 8,90,043 tiles in the month of July. Out of these 8,85,178 tiles were found good in the quality check. How many tiles were defective?

A) 4865   B) 3500   C) 5555   D) 8564

7. What could be the number in the END box?

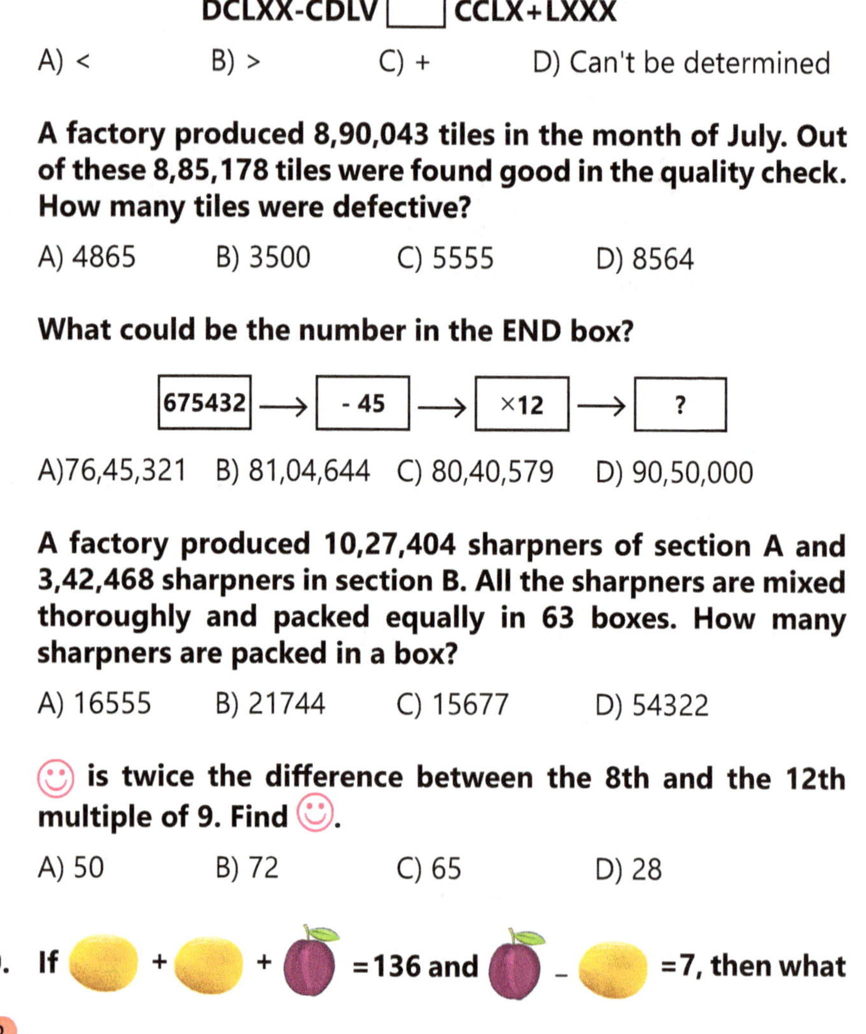

A)76,45,321   B) 81,04,644   C) 80,40,579   D) 90,50,000

8. A factory produced 10,27,404 sharpners of section A and 3,42,468 sharpners in section B. All the sharpners are mixed thoroughly and packed equally in 63 boxes. How many sharpners are packed in a box?

A) 16555   B) 21744   C) 15677   D) 54322

9. ☺ **is twice the difference between the 8th and the 12th multiple of 9. Find** ☺**.**

A) 50   B) 72   C) 65   D) 28

10. If 🍋 **+** 🍋 **+** 🫐 **= 136 and** 🫐 **−** 🍋 **= 7, then what**

is the value of 🍑 ?

A) 85   B) 40   C) 75   D) 50

11. **What must be subtracted from 1 lakh to get 75413?**

A) 84587   B) 76990   C) 79813   D) 24587

12. **The value of $15 \times 6 + 48 \div 6 + 14 = $______.**

A) 343   B) 127   C) 112   D) 155

13. **Highest common factor of 84 and 144 is ______.**

A) 12   B) 8   C) 2   D) 3

14. **The number of prime factors of 20 are ______.**

A) 8   B) 2   C) 4   D) 1

15. **Find the estimated sum of 4,25,622 and 1,59,912 by rounding off the result to the nearest hundreds.**

A) 5,85,600   B) 5,85,500   C) 5,86,000   D) 5,00,500

16. **In a office, there are 588 chairs to be placed in 14 departments, if the same number of chairs are placed in each department, then how many chairs will be there in each department?**

A) 42   B) 29   C) 84   D) 16

17. **The sum of 2nd multiple of 2 and 8th multiple of 8 is divisible by ______.**

A) 5   B) 9   C) 7   D) 2

18. **Which of the following could be solved by using sentences A - 5?**

A)   Akshay is 5 times as old as Vijay. If A is Vijay's age in years, then how old is Akshay?

B)   Tina is 5 years younger than Anjali. If A is Anjali's age in years, then how old is Tina?

C) Niraj is one-fifth as old as Om. If A is Niraj's age in years, how old is Om?

D) Gayatri is 5 years older than Swapnali. If A is Swapnali's age in year's, then how old is Gayatri?

19. The quotient when 54,67,812 is divided by 28 is______.

A) 1,00,000   B) 1,95,279   C) 10,60,008   D) 1,89,459

20. A cloth store to sold 214532 dresses in the year 2018 : 12675 dresses in the year 2019 and 319067 dresses in the year 2020. What was the total number of dresses sold in all three years?

A) 5,46,274   B) 5,33,074   C) 4,00,000   D) 5,46,000

EVERYDAY MATHEMATICS

21. In a certain area, 9089752 people were working in various companies. Of these 1478123 people work in Tata company, 1878543 people work in Indira pvt Ltd and the rest in Durga company. How many people work in Durga company?

A) 25,58,906   B) 38,54,543   C) 10,55,090   D) 22,21,976

22. 5412 boxes of toys were stored in a godown. If each box contained 57 toys, then find the total number of toys stored in the godown.

A) 3,00,000   B) 3,08,484   C) 2,26,340   D) 6,56,459

23. A XYZ earned ₹ 47,89,000 in a year. If the total expenses were ₹ 2,76,894, then how much money was saved?

A) ₹ 1,12,675   B) ₹ 25,22,124   C) ₹ 41,15,005   D) ₹ 45,12,106

24. A contractor sent 6785431 bricks for the construction of 17 chambers. If an equal number sof bricks were required for each chamber, then how many bricks were used for each chamber?

A) 88,671   B) 2,29,863   C) 5,78,903   D) 3,99,143

25. Each floor of a building has 20 windows. There are 12 floors in each building. There are 25 such building in a complex. Calculate the total number of windows in the complex.

A) 8380   B) 5580   C) 6000   D) 2460

ACHIEVERS SECTION (HOTS)

26. Find the value of P - Q + S + P.

A) 9

B) 22

C) 18

D) 16

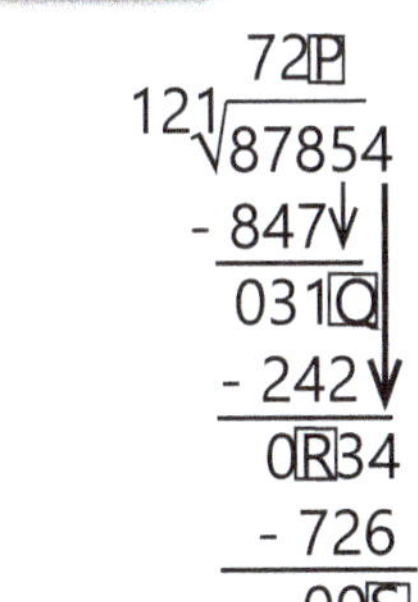

27. A total of 18816 chairs were arranged in the offices, cultural department and halls of all floor in a building. Each floors had 2 offices, 1 cultural department, 2 halls. The number of chairs used are given below:

1 office =64 chairs, 1 cultural department =84 chairs and 1 halls =52 chairs

How many floors are there in the building?

A) 84   B) 92   C) 56   D) 82

28. Company P can produce 8200 packets of snacks in a day, Which is 135 fewer than what company Q can produce in a day. Now, 35 packets of snacks are packed in a box. If both company P and Q are used, then how many such packets of snacks will be there after 7 days?

A) 7654   B) 1231   C) 5342   D) 3305

29. Vicky's balance in a bank on 1st June was ₹ 45,830. He deposits ₹ 2130 and ₹ 22280 in his account and withdrew

₹ 58,630 from his account in that month. What was the balance at the end of the month?

A) ₹ 15800   B) ₹ 9700   C) ₹ 50200   D) ₹ 11,610

30. Find the value of (A+B) – (C+D) by completing the given addition matrix.

+	8670	12890
15470	A	B
6790	C	D

A) 17760   B) 20120   C) 11209   D) 13450

FRACTION AND DECIMALS

* Fractional or decimal form of shaded and unshaded parts
* Simplification of fraction in simplest form
* Equivalent fractions
* Compare fractional number or decimal number, arranging in ascending and descending order
* Improper fractions and mixed fractions
* Fractions represented in the form of whole
* Express fractions in decimal number form and decimal numbers in fractional form
* Rounding off decimal numbers to the nearest ten's, hundred's, thousand's , tenths, hundredths and thousandths
* Operations on fractions
* Word problems on fractions and decimals

MATHEMATICAL REASONING

1. **What is the sum of the shaded fractions of the given figures?**

   A) $\dfrac{27}{40}$ B) $\dfrac{15}{20}$

   C) $\dfrac{13}{40}$ D) $\dfrac{20}{13}$

   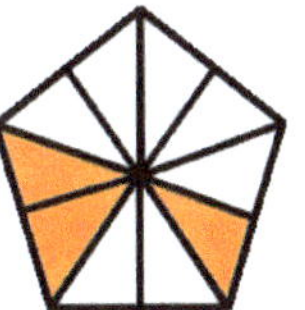 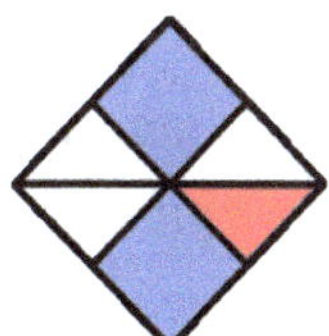

2. **In the product of 48.77 and 6, find the place value of digit 6.**

   A) 0.06   B) 0.60   C) 60   D) 2

3. **Hema distributed ₹ 54.39 among her seven cousins. If she distributes ₹ 37.72 to her six cousins, then how much money did she gave to her seventh cousin?**

   A) ₹ 16.67   B) ₹ 18.00   C) ₹ 88.34   D) ₹ 34.20

4. **What is 3578.398 rounded off to the nearest tenths?**

   A) 4000.00   B) 3578.40   C) 3500   D) 3578.4

5. **Which of the following decimals are arranged in decending order?**

   A) 33.4, 33.006, 33.41   B) 14.22, 14.1, 14.001

   C) 0.90, 90.00, 9.00   D) 6.002, 6.00, 00.66

6. **On sports day, Aryan jumped $4\frac{7}{12}$ feet and Ram jumped $3\frac{1}{6}$ feet. How much father did Aryan jump than Ram?**

   A) 4 feet   B) $1\frac{5}{8}$ feet   C) $1\frac{5}{12}$ feet   D) $\frac{5}{12}$ feet

7. **The sum of (4 tens and 10 hundredths) and (60 tens and 8 tenths) is _______.**

   A) 980.4   B) 240.0   C) 340.6   D) 640.9

8. **Minal bought a cake. She gave $\frac{1}{6}$ of the cake to each of her four friends. What fraction of the cake is left with her?**

   A) $\frac{2}{6}$ B) $\frac{1}{5}$ C) $\frac{3}{4}$ D) $\frac{1}{8}$

9. **What is the value of (482.20+726.44) when rounded of to nearest tenths?**

   A) 1208.00   B) 1208.64   C) 1208.6   D) 1200.60

10. **Find the value of X.**

X	$\xrightarrow{+5}$	9.15	$\xrightarrow{\times 2}$	18.3	$\xrightarrow{+4}$	22.3

   A) 4.55   B) 9.65   C) 4.15   D) 1.20

11. **What fraction of the given figure is shaded?**

A) $\dfrac{1}{2}$

B) $\dfrac{4}{7}$

C) $\dfrac{3}{4}$

D) $\dfrac{6}{4}$

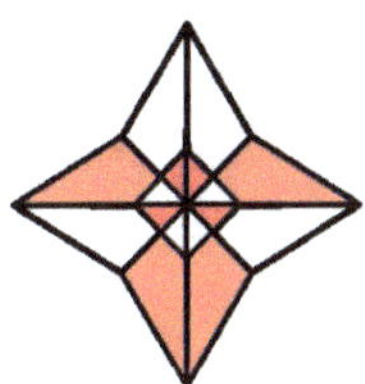

12. Which of the following shows the equivalent fraction of $\dfrac{2}{4}$?

A) $\dfrac{8}{12}$　　B) $\dfrac{8}{16}$　　C) $\dfrac{12}{24}$　　D) $\dfrac{24}{40}$

13. How many of the shapes of the given figure must be shaded so that $\dfrac{2}{5}$ of the figure is unshaded?

A) 8

B) 12

C) 15

D) 22

14. Anita think of a decimal number. After I have subtracted 2.9 from it, multiplied the result by 3 and then added 0.15, I get 10.5. what decimal number Anita is thinking of?

A) 5.9　　B) 10.55　　C) 20.10　　D) 6.35

15. What must be added $2\dfrac{2}{5}$ to give $3\dfrac{3}{10}$?

A) $\dfrac{9}{10}$　　B) $\dfrac{5}{6}$　　C) $1\dfrac{3}{10}$　　D) $1\dfrac{5}{5}$

16. Which of the following fractions are in order from the least to the greatest?

A) $\dfrac{2}{6}, \dfrac{2}{3}, \dfrac{1}{2}$　　　　B) $\dfrac{1}{2}, \dfrac{2}{3}, \dfrac{2}{6}$

C) $\dfrac{1}{2}, \dfrac{2}{6}, \dfrac{2}{3}$　　　　D) $\dfrac{2}{6} \cdot \dfrac{1}{2}, \dfrac{2}{3}$

17. What is the missing value in the given mathematical statement?

$$0.25 \times 12 = 0.25 \times 3 + 0.25 \times 3 + 0.25 \times \boxed{?}$$

A) 8   B) 4   C) 6   D) 2

18. **Find the missing value.**

$$2.25 + 9 + 1\frac{1}{8} - (6.5 \times 0.2) = \underline{\quad ? \quad} \times \frac{1}{4}$$

A) 1.3   B) 0.3   C) 0.0072   D) 1.735

19. **Divide 24.28 by the difference of 98 tenths and 580 hundredths.**

A) 6.07   B) 8.45   C) 5.20   D) 7.91

20. **Which of the following options is correct?**

A) 1.4589 < 1.0488   B) 1.8764 < 1.9801

C) 1.980 < 1.4676   D) 1.463 < 1.2897

EVERYDAY MATHEMATICS

21. **Aisha takes $\frac{1}{8}$ hour to walk to the garden and $\frac{1}{4}$ hour to walk from the garden to home. How much time does it take her to walk to the garden and then to home?**

A) $\frac{2}{2}$ hour   B) $\frac{2}{12}$ hour   C) $\frac{1}{2}$ hour   D) $\frac{2}{3}$ hour

22. **Ram packed $\frac{3}{4}$ kg of rice each into 42 bags. Find the total weight of rice Ram packed.**

A) 32.5 kg   B) 335 kg   C) 31.5 kg   D) 3.45 kg

23. **In a fair Ragini and Diya spent ₹ 95 together Diya and Deepa spent ₹ 216 together. If Diya spent $\frac{1}{5}$ of what Deepa spent, then how much did Ragini spend?**

A) ₹ 59   B) ₹ 62   C) ₹ 75   D) ₹ 89

24. **Anuja have to multiply 24.22 by 4. Instead, she multiply 2.422 by 7. What is the difference between the two answers?**

A) 115.26   B) 87.192   C) 98.22   D) 110.323

25. Amruta work on her project $7\frac{1}{2}$ hours a week. If she work $1\frac{1}{2}$ hours each day, then how many days does she work each week?

A) 5   B) 7   C) 9   D) 4

26. Evaluate: $\dfrac{2\frac{5}{4} - 5\frac{1}{6} + 3\frac{1}{3}}{0.087 + 0.3717 + 0.9}$

A) 2.833   B) 0.00028   C) 0.28   D) 0.000028

27. The value of 30.5 – 30.4 + 30.3 - 30.2 + 30.1 - 30.0 + 29.9 - 29.8 + 29.7 - 29.6 + 29.5 – 29.4 + 29.3 – 29.2 + 29.1 - 29.0 = ______.

A) 0.8   B) 0.5   C) 1.8   D) 0.08

28. Find the value of P, Q, R and S respectively.

Figure	Shaded	
	Fraction	Decimal
	P	Q
	R	S

A) $1\frac{2}{5}$, 1.4, $2\frac{1}{2}$, 2.5   B) $1\frac{3}{5}$, 1.6, $2\frac{1}{2}$, 2.5

C) $1\frac{2}{5}$, 1.4, $3\frac{1}{2}$, 2.5   D) $1\frac{3}{5}$, 1.6, $3\frac{1}{2}$, 3.5

29. Which of the following statements is CORRECT?

A) $\frac{3}{6}$ and $\frac{1}{2}$ are equivalent fractions.

B) 1 mm is $\dfrac{1}{100}$ of 1 cm

C) $\dfrac{1}{2}$ of an hour is equal to 20 minutes.

D) $\dfrac{5}{6}$ is equal to $\dfrac{6}{5}$

30. Find the value of R - P + Q

(i) 231.22 + 7.4 = P

(ii) Q + 6.32 = 18.65

(iii) 871.09 – R = 396.02

A) 579.32   B) 356.23   C) 248.78   D) 445.87

Colour your choice with color pencil				
1	**2**	**3**	**4**	**5**
A B C D	A B C D	A B C D	A B C D	A B C D
6	**7**	**8**	**9**	**10**
A B C D	A B C D	A B C D	A B C D	A B C D
11	**12**	**13**	**14**	**15**
A B C D	A B C D	A B C D	A B C D	A B C D
16	**17**	**18**	**19**	**20**
A B C D	A B C D	A B C D	A B C D	A B C D
21	**22**	**23**	**24**	**25**
A B C D	A B C D	A B C D	A B C D	A B C D
26	**27**	**28**	**29**	**30**
A B C D	A B C D	A B C D	A B C D	A B C D

CHAPTER 4

MEASUREMENTS

* Conversion of units from one unit to another
* Word problems on measuring units (Temperature, Time, Lenght, Weight, Capacity and Money)

MATHEMATICAL REASONING

1. **5 cups of wheat of the same weight weighs 690 g. 1 glass of wheat weighs 200 g. How much heavier is 1 glass of wheat than 1 cup of wheat?**

   A) 90 g   B) 220 g   C) 340 g   D) 62 g

2. **The given clock shows the time at which the dance program finished in the evening. If the program was 3 hrs 20 minutes long and there was a break of 20 minutes in between, then at what time did the program starts?**

   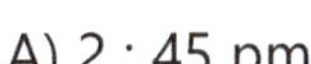

   A) 2 : 45 pm   B) 1 : 35 pm

   C) 2 : 40 pm   D) 2 : 55 pm

3. **Express $5\frac{2}{3}$ hrs in minutes.**

   A) 280 mins   B) 259 mins   C) 340 mins   D) 390 mins

4. **Pool P contains 5 times as much water as Pool Q. How much water must be transfer from Pool P to Pool Q so that each Pool contains 45 litres of water?**

   A) 30 litres   B) 40 litres   C) 75 litres   D) 55 litres

5. A water pool can hold $49\frac{5}{6}$ liters of water. How much water will be contained in 3 such pools?

A) $132\frac{4}{3}$ litres

B) $149\frac{1}{2}$ litres

C) 82 litres

D) 120 litres

6. What temperature does the given thermometer shows?

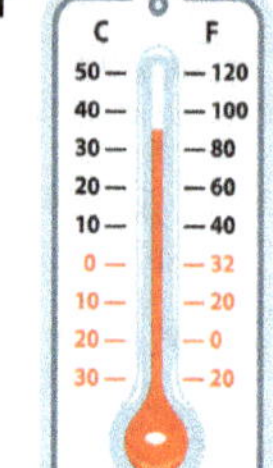

A) 35°C

B) 75°C

C) 93°F

D) 124°F

7. A wall is painted green and orange. The green portion is 1.8 m long, and the orange portion is three times as long as the green portion. What is the lenght of wall?

A) 4.1 m   B) 7.2 m   C) 6.8 m   D) None of these

8. The given figure shows two crayons. What is the sum of length of both the crayons?

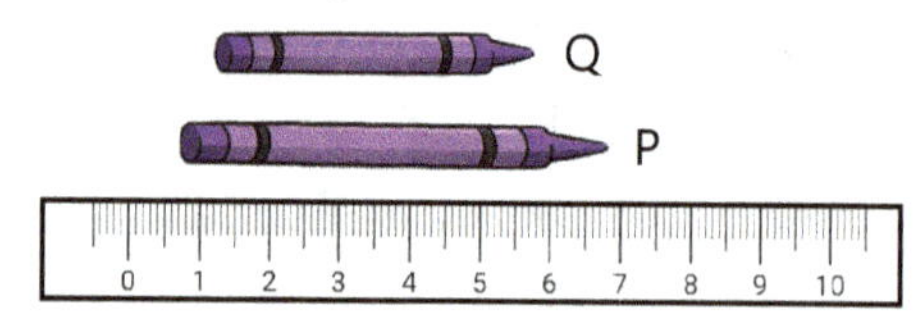

A) 11.66 m   B) 10.6 m   C) 12.4 m   D) 10.8 m

9. At 10 p.m., the temperature was 32°C. After one hour, it had gone up by 7°C, and then after every one hour, it had gone down by 3°C. What was the temperature at 1 a.m?

A) 30°C   B) 46°C   C) 33°C   D) 38°C

10. How long did Komal work in kitchen?

Started working

Stopped working

A) 120 minutes

B) 40 minutes

C) 2 hour

D) 1 hour 41 minutes

DIRECTION (11-12): The given table shows the cost of watch and pair of shoes at three different shops, Study it carefully and answer the questions that follows.

	Shop X	Shop Y	Shop Z
Watch	2 for ₹ 1500	3 for ₹ 2100	1 for ₹ 600
Pair of Shoes	1 for ₹ 900	2 for ₹ 1700	3 for ₹ 2100

11. **Which of the following two shops sell the watch at same price?**

A) X and Y   B) X and Z   C) Y and Z   D) None of these

12. **If Mayur bought two pair of shoes and 1 watch from shop Y, then find the total amount spend by him.**

A) ₹ 2400   B) ₹ 1900   C) ₹ 2255   D) ₹ 2700

13. **The height of a table is thrice the height of chair. If the height of the table is 1 m 14 cm, then find the height of the chair.**

A) 0.38 m   B) 38 m   C) 03.8 m   D) 3.80 cm

14. **If** P Q **18 kg and** P P **16 kg then find**

weight of Q**.**

A) 5 kg   B) 10 kg   C) 3 kg   D) 8 kg

15. If A = (6.8 × 4.2) m and B is 4 m less than A, then what is the length of B?

A) 32.5 m   B) 39.5 m   C) 27.59 m   D) 24.56 m

EVERYDAY MATHEMATICS

16. Kranti made 4.8 L of juice. Mrunal made thrice as much juice as Kranti made. How much juice did they make together?

A) 18.6 L   B) 19.2 L   C) 20.6 L   D) 33.5 L

17. The given table shows the prices of 3 different types of cupcakes. $\frac{1}{4}$ of the cupcakes Deepti bought were egg cupcakes. $\frac{1}{8}$ of them were strawberry cupcakes and the rest were mango cupcakes. If Deepti spent a total amount of ₹ 6.50 on the egg and strawberry cupcakes, then how much did she spend on the mango cupcakes?

Egg cupcakes	20 paise each
Stawberry cupcakes	90 paise each
Mango cupcakes	5 paise each

A) ₹ 1.25   B) ₹ 1.50   C) ₹ 1.70   D) ₹ 1.90

18. Anjali pours 1 L 950 ml of milk equally into 5 glasses. How much milk is there in each glass?

A) 500 ml   B) 400 ml   C) 390 ml   D) 120 ml

19. A coffee mug holds 1 L 440 ml of coffee. If a small coffee cup of capacity 90 ml is used to serve, then for how many people coffee can be served?

A) 15   B) 12   C) 16   D) 18

20. Mayuri had 480 kg of sweets. She packed $\frac{3}{8}$ of it into a

sweets container and packed $\frac{3}{5}$ of the remaining equally into 6 boxes. How much sweets was there in each box?

A) 50 kg   B) 20 kg   C) 30 kg   D) 45 kg

21. The cost of 1 kg of tomatos and 1 kg of cucumbers are ₹ 29.85 and ₹ 38.80 respectively.

    If Dipesh bought 3 kg tomato and 5 kg cucumber, then find the total amount paid by him.

    A) ₹ 190.20   B) ₹ 283   C) ₹ 320   D) ₹ 283.55

22. Snehal had 17.85 m of lace. She cut 9 smaller pieces each of length 0.35 m from it. How many meters of lace were left?

    A) 13.7 m   B) 14.7 m   C) 8.90 m   D) 19.5 m

23. 520 g of red jelly beans are mixed with 580 g of blue jelly beans and packed into 5 equal packets. How many grams of the mixture are there in each packet?

    A) 220 g   B) 340 g   C) 240 g   D) 170 g

24. Raghav had a sheet of paper. He cut 3 smaller pieces of paper each $\frac{3}{4}$ m from it. If he had left with $5\frac{3}{4}$ of paper, then find the total length of the paper.

    A) 2 m   B) 5 m   C) 8 m   D) 4 m

25. Swapnil drive a car 125.20 km on Saturday and 47.65 km on Sunday. How many less kilometers did he drive on Sunday than on Saturday?

    A) 77.55 km   B) 42.30 km   C) 62.70 km   D) 72.89 km

ACHIEVERS SECTION (HOTS)

26. Asha made 16.5 L of lemonade. Swapna made 3.5 L more lemonade than Asha. Swapna sold $\frac{3}{4}$ of her lemonade. If

Asha had left with half of lemonade that of Swapna left, then how much lemonade did Asha sold?

A) 14 L   B) 12.5 L   C) 19 L   D) 17.5 L

27. The length of a red garland 2 m 98 cm long, is half as long as a yellow garland. Ankita used $1\frac{2}{5}$ m of the yellow garland to decorate the wall, she then cut the rest of yellow garland into 4 small pieces of equal length. What is he length of each small piece?

A) 119 m   B) 0.25 m   C) 1.14 m   D) 29 m

28.
then what is the weight of R ?

A) 4 kg   B) 5 kg   C) 8 kg   D) 7 kg

29. The given table shows the weights of some balls. What is the weight of ball P?

Balls	P Q Q	Q R S	P S R
Weight(in g)	660	600	540

A) 120 g   B) 290 g   C) 180 g   D) 250 g

30.

A) $\frac{5}{4}$ kg   B) $1\frac{7}{8}$ kg   C) $\frac{8}{9}$ kg   D) $1\frac{5}{4}$ kg

ANGLES

* Concept of Parallel, Perpendicular and Intersecting lines
* Types of Angles
* Measurement of Angles
* Reading of an angle formed by the hands of a clock

MATHEMATICAL REASONING

1. **When it is 03:05, what kind of angle is formed by the hands of the clock as shown in the given clock?**

   A) Obtuse

   B) Acute

   C) Right

   D) Straight

   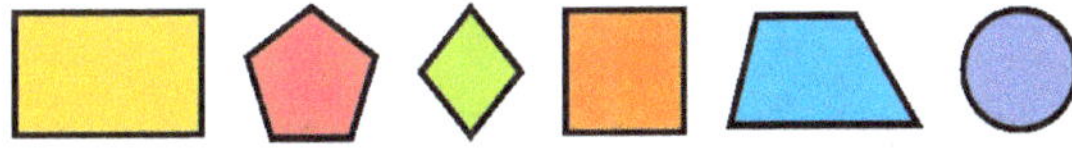

2. **How many of the following figures have parallel lines?**

   A) 4

   B) 3

   C) 2

   D) 5

3. **At what time given below do the minutes and hour hands of a clock make a right angle?**

   A) 6 O'clock

   B) 3 O'clock

   C) 4 O'clock

   D) 12 O'clock

4. **How many pairs of perpendicular lines are there in the given figure?**

   A) 2

   B) 4

   C) 0

   D) 5

   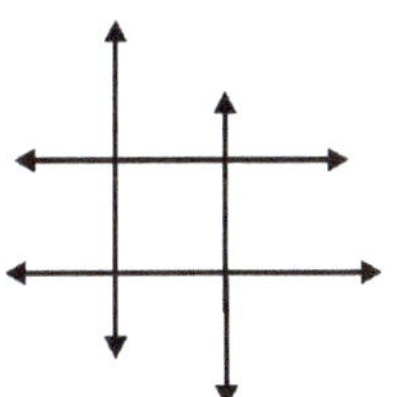

5. **How many angles inside the given figure are right angles?**

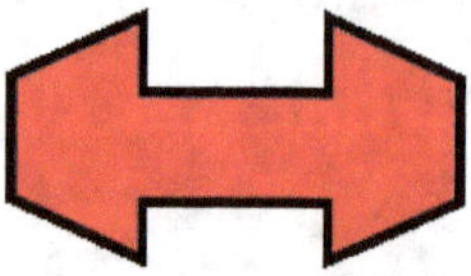

A) 4

B) 5

C) 0

D) 3

6. **Four pupils each made a statement about the given figure.**

Swati : I can see 4 pairs of acute angles.

Varsha : There are 7 angles in the figure.

Riya : There are two pairs of parallel lines

Harish : 4 of the acute angles are less than a right angle.

Which pupils makes the correct statement?

A) Swati   B) Varsha   C) Harish   D) Riya

7. **An angle which measure 90° is called _____ angle.**

A) Straight   B) Obtuse   C) Acute   D) Right

8. **How many of the given letters have parallel lines?**

ANGLE

A) 3   B) 2   C) 4   D) 1

9. **Which of the following is NOT drawn in the given figure?**

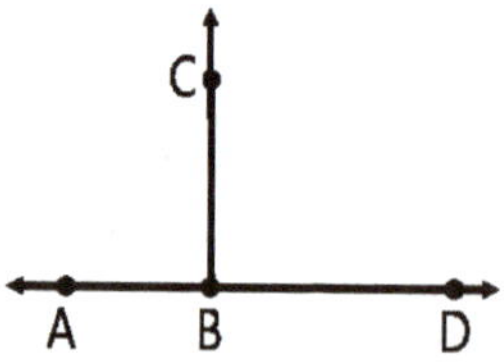

A) Angle B

B) Ray BD

C) Line AD

D) Line segment CD

10. **The angle in the given clock shows_____ angle.**

A) Acute   B) Straight

C) Reflex   D) Obtuse

11. **Rohit drew an angle that was half the measure of angle shown the figure. What type of angle did Rohit drew?**

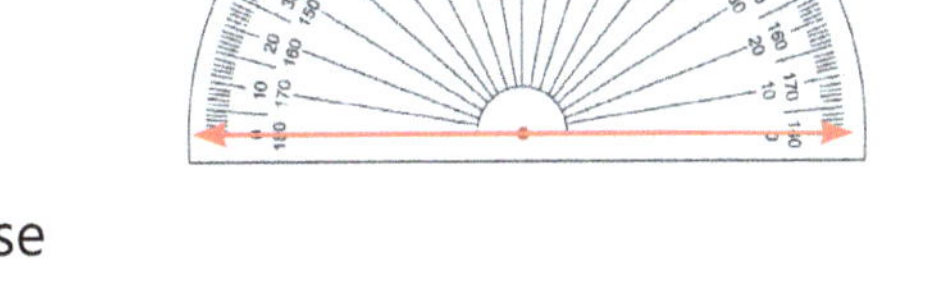

A) Acute　　　B) Right

C) Obtuse　　D) None of these

12. **A 10 : 15, the angle formed between the two hands of clock is _______.**

A) Acute　　　B) Obtuse　　　C) Right　　　D) None of these

13. **How many of the given figures have perpendicular lines?**

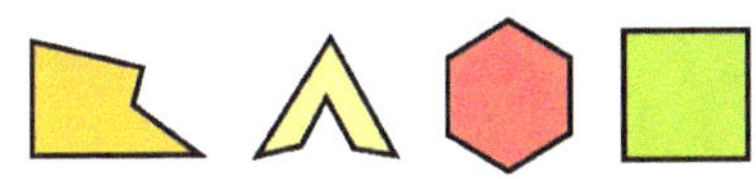

A) 4　　　　　B) 2　　　　　C) 1　　　　　D) 3

14. **Which type of angle best describes angle Q?**

A) Right　　　　　　　　B) Straight

C) Obtuse　　　　　　　D) Acute

15. **How many angles are more than 90° in the given figure?**

A) 2　　　　　　　　　B) 4

C) 0　　　　　　　　　D) 3

16. **An angle which measures less than 90° is called a/an _____ angle.**

A) Obtuse　　　B) Acute　　　C) Right　　　D) None of these

17. **In the given figure, which line is no intersecting to AB?**

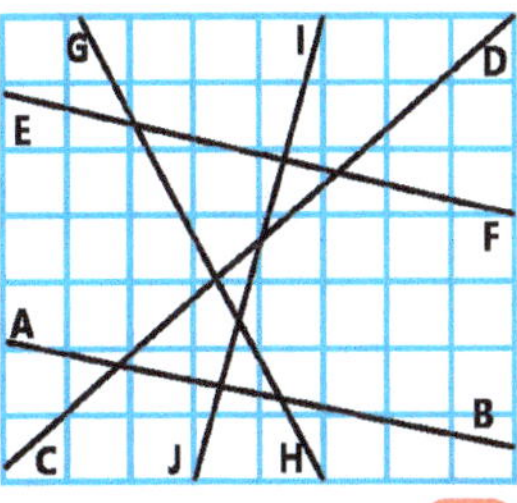

A) GH　　　　　　　B) EF

C) CD　　　　　　　D) IJ

18. **Which of the following angle is less than a right angle?**

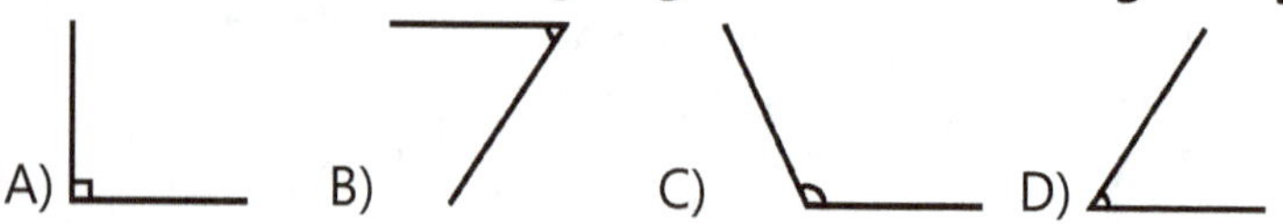

A)   B)   C)   D)

19. **What is the approximate measure of the angle shown in the given figure?**

A) 20°   B) 110°

C) 45°   D) 135°

20. **There are six angles given below. How many of them are more than a right angle.**

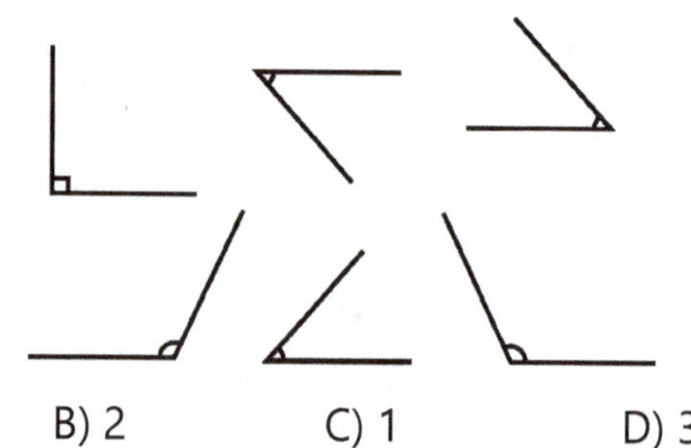

A) 4   B) 2   C) 1   D) 3

ACHIEVERS SECTION (HOTS)

21. **The number of acute angles in the given figure is ___.**

A) 6   B) 5

C) 7   D) 4

22. **Which of the following statements is INCORRECT about the given figure?**

A) The figure has 3 acute angles.

B) The figure has 2 right angles.

C) The figure has 4 obtuse angles.

D) None of these

23. How many angles in the given figure are more than 90°?

A) 14 B) 13

C) 15 D) 12

24. There are ___ pairs of intersecting lines in the given figure.

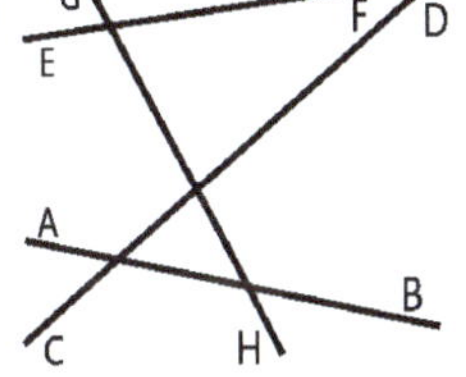

A) 3 B) 5

C) 2 D) 4

25. How many obtuse angles are there on the outside of the figure shown below?

A) 4 B) 6

C) 2 D) 5

<table>
<tr><td colspan="5" align="center">Colour your choice with color pencil</td></tr>
<tr><td>1</td><td>2</td><td>3</td><td>4</td><td>5</td></tr>
<tr><td>A B C D</td><td>A B C D</td><td>A B C D</td><td>A B C D</td><td>A B C D</td></tr>
<tr><td>6</td><td>7</td><td>8</td><td>9</td><td>10</td></tr>
<tr><td>A B C D</td><td>A B C D</td><td>A B C D</td><td>A B C D</td><td>A B C D</td></tr>
<tr><td>11</td><td>12</td><td>13</td><td>14</td><td>15</td></tr>
<tr><td>A B C D</td><td>A B C D</td><td>A B C D</td><td>A B C D</td><td>A B C D</td></tr>
<tr><td>16</td><td>17</td><td>18</td><td>19</td><td>20</td></tr>
<tr><td>A B C D</td><td>A B C D</td><td>A B C D</td><td>A B C D</td><td>A B C D</td></tr>
<tr><td>21</td><td>22</td><td>23</td><td>24</td><td>25</td></tr>
<tr><td>A B C D</td><td>A B C D</td><td>A B C D</td><td>A B C D</td><td>A B C D</td></tr>
</table>

PERIMETER AND AREA

* Perimeter of polygons
* Area of squares and rectangle
* Finding perimeter and area by counting the number of squares

MATHEMATICAL REASONING

1. **A mat is laid on the floor of a room 8 m by 5 m, leaving a border 0.5 m wide all round it. What is the perimeter of the carpet?**

   A) 22 m   B) 28 m   C) 26 m   D) 24 m

2. **What is the area if the given figure?**

   A) 15 square units

   B) 45 square units

   C) 22 square units

   D) 20 square units

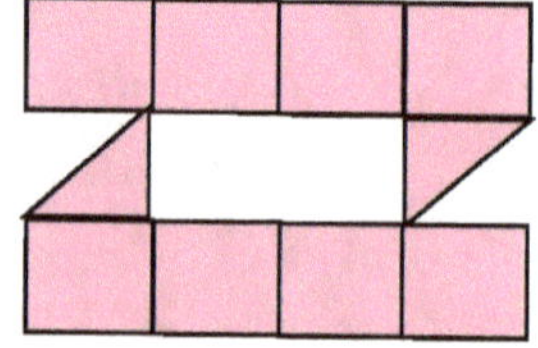

3. **The figure is made up of 8 identical square. Find total area of the shaded figure.**

   A) 200 sq. cm

   B) 150 sq. cm

   C) 300 sq. cm

   D) 100 sq. cm

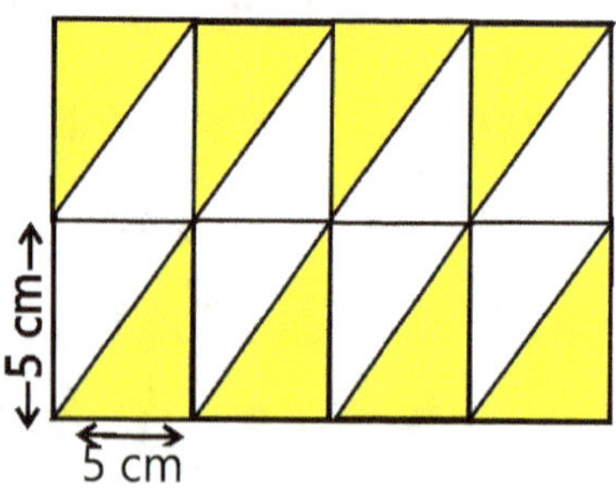

4. **Find the perimeter of the given figure (not drawn of scale).**

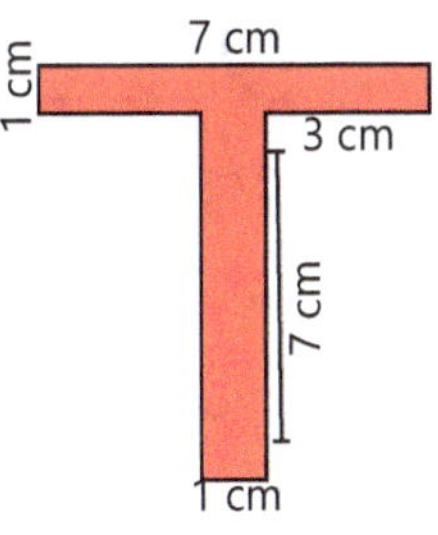

A) 49 cm

B) 50 cm

C) 30 cm

D) 45 cm

5. **PRTV is square (not drawn to scale). PQ is thrice of QR. If QS = UW = 5 cm, then find the perimeter of WPQSTU.**

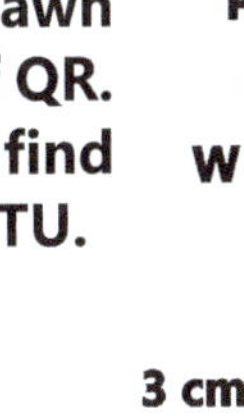

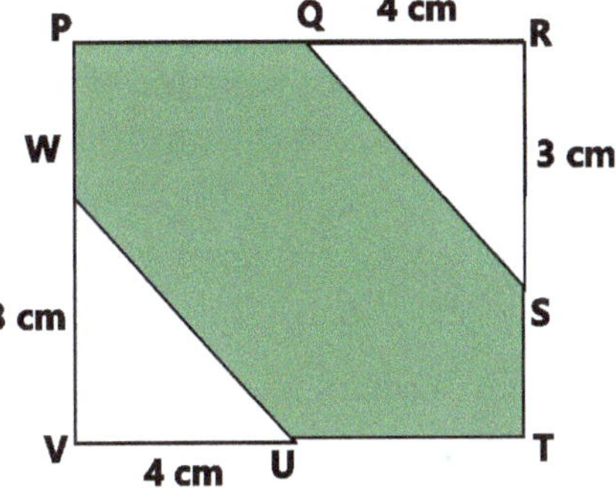

A) 60 cm

B) 50 cm

C) 45 cm

D) 48 cm

6. **What is the area of the shaded figure?**

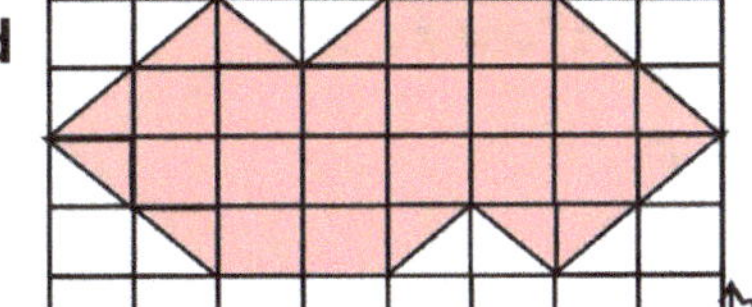

A) 210 sq. cm   B) 55 sq. cm

C) 88 sq. cm   D) 120 sq. cm

7. **Perimeter of any regular figure is___.**

A) Sum of its all sides

B) Product of its all sides

C) Both (A) and (B)

D) None of these

8. **The perimeter of a rectangular TV screen is 180 cm. Its is 60 cm long. Find the width of the TV screen.**

A) 80 cm   B) 20 cm   C) 30 cm   D) 45 cm

9. **Find the total shaded area of the figure made up of identical squares.**

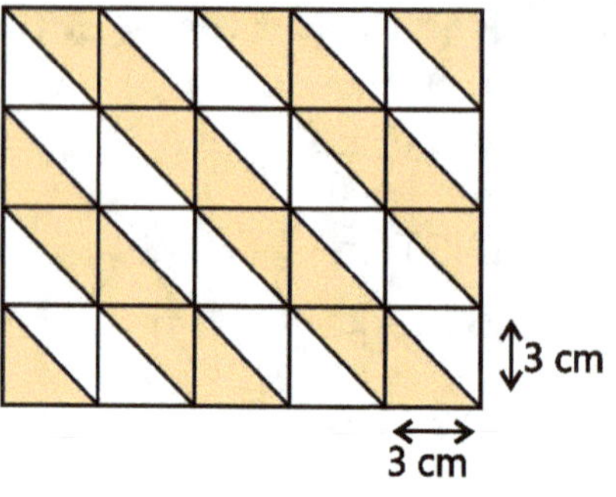

A) 85 sq. cm

B) 80 sq. cm

C) 90 sq. cm

D) 98 sq. cm

10. **Find the perimeter of the given figure (not drawn to scale).**

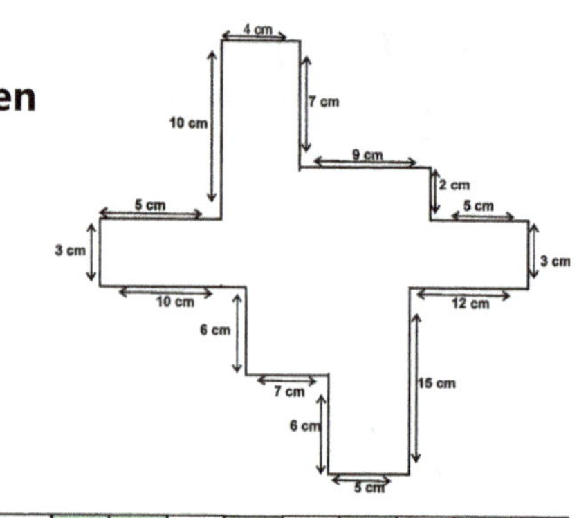

A) 130 cm

B) 96 cm

C) 109 cm

D) 115 cm

11. **Which shape has the smallest area?**

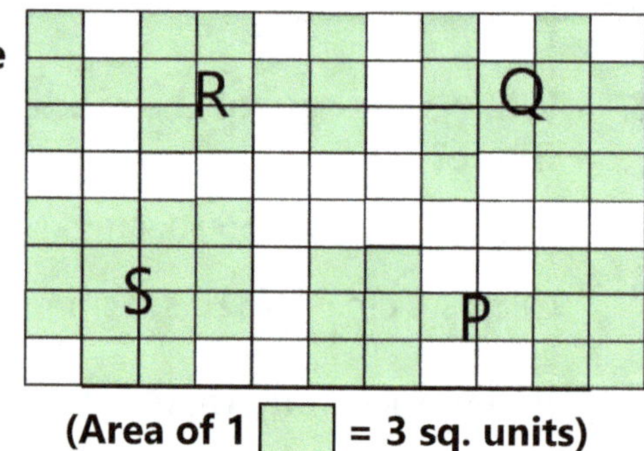

A) Q

B) S

C) P

D) R

(Area of 1 ☐ = 3 sq. units)

12. **Find the total area of the shaded parts of the rectangle PQRT (not drawn to scale).**

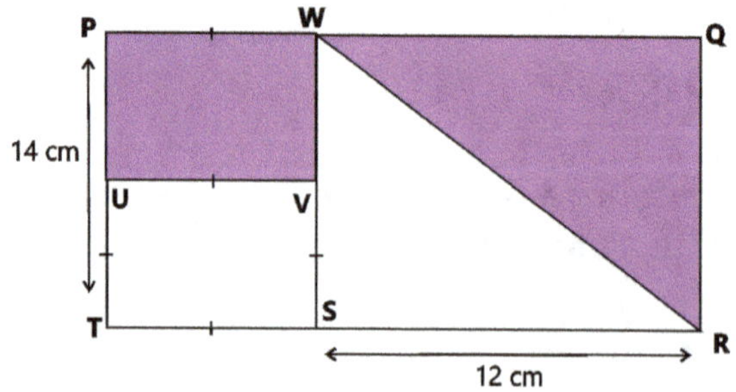

A) 120 sq. cm B) 140 sq. cm

C) 145 sq. cm D) 133 sq. cm

13. **The given figure (not drawn to scale) is made up of two squares. Find its total area.**

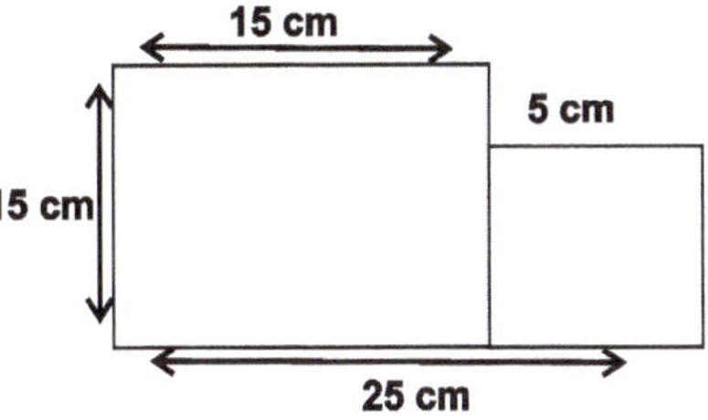

A) 150 sq. cm B) 325 sq. cm

C) 155 sq. cm D) 311 sq. cm

14. **Find the area if the shaded figure.**

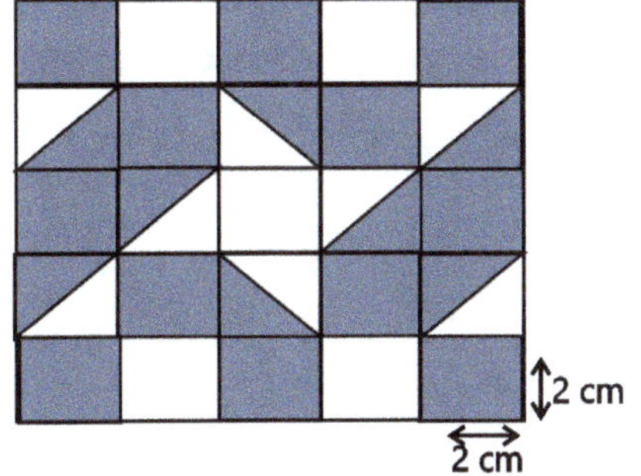

A) 64 sq. cm

B) 50 sq. cm

C) 40 sq. cm

D) 50 sq. cm

15. **Find the perimeter of the given figure (not drawn to scale).**

A) 92 cm

B) 105 cm

C) 60 cm

D) 75 cm

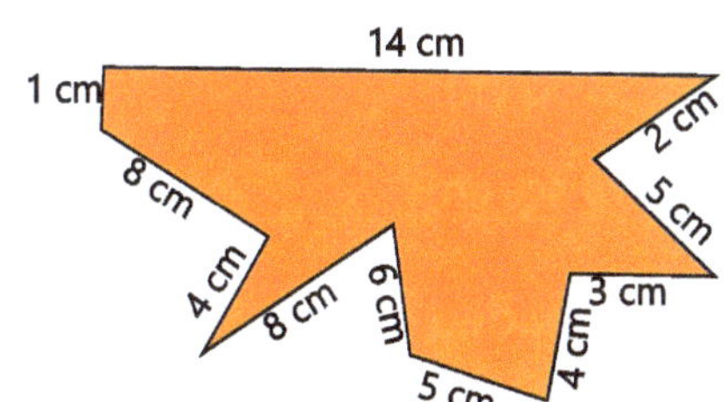

16. **PQRS is a rectangle (not drawn to scale) of perimeter 28 m. Two rectangle corners have been cut away as shown in the figure. What is the perimeter of the shaded figure?**

A) 22 m

B) 24 m

C) 28 m

D) 30 m

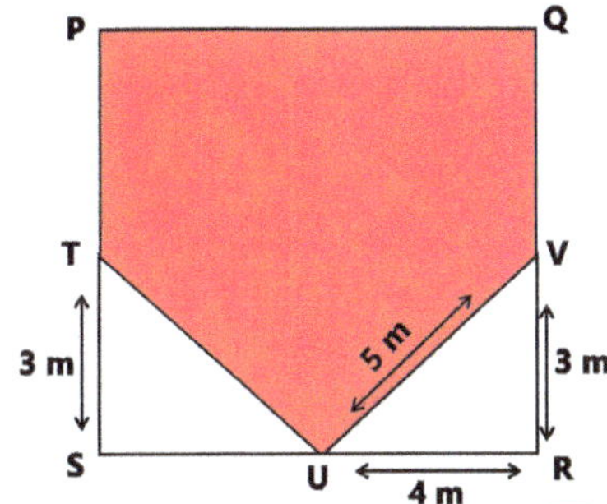

17. **In the given figure (not drawn to scale), ABCD is a square and unshaded parts are rectangles.**

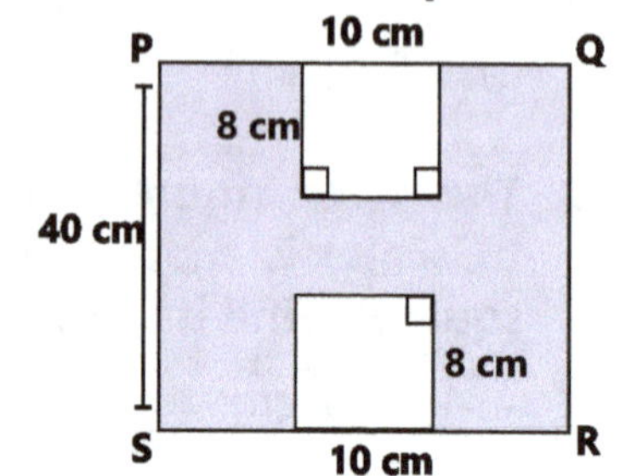

A) 1000 sq. cm

B) 1210 sq. cm

C) 1540 sq. cm

D) 1440 sq. cm

18. **The figure given below is made up of 4 similar squares and 2 triangles. The perimeter of each square is 32 cm. What is the perimeter of the figure?**

A) 102 cm   B) 176 cm

C) 120 cm   D) 112 cm

19. **Find the area of the shaded part in the given figure (not drawn to scale).**

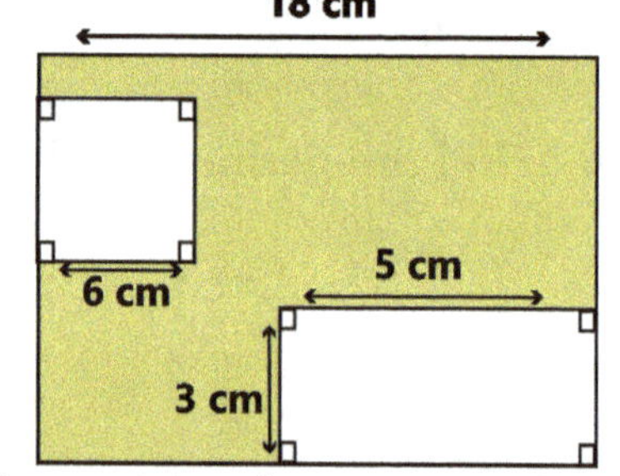

A) 45 sq. cm

B) 39 sq. cm

C) 58 sq.cm

D) 93 sq. cm

20.. **The shaded part in the given figure (not drawn to scale) is covered with colour. If it costs ₹ 70 to colour an area of 2 sq. cm. then find the total cost of coloring.**

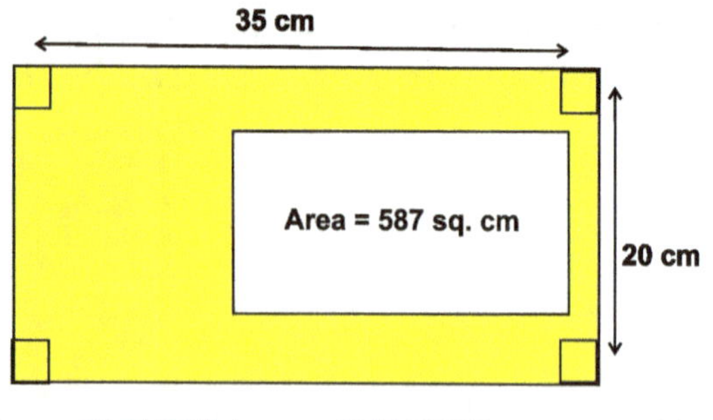

A) ₹ 3955   B) ₹ 2954   C) ₹ 3775   D) ₹ 5550

21. **Ajay's family is planning to build a swimming pool in their backyard. How many square meters will be left in the backyard for grass?**

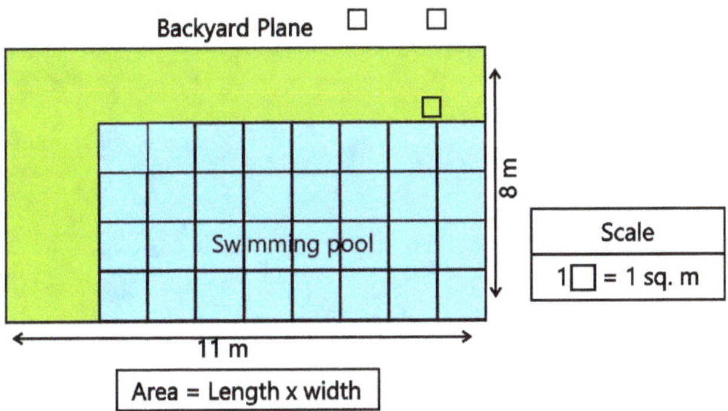

A) 24 sq. cm   B) 60 sq. cm   C) 31 sq. cm   D) 35 sq. cm

22. **The area of the rectangle wall is 90 sq. m. What is it perimeter if its length is 20 m?**

A) 18 m   B) 55 m   C) 82 m   D) 75 m

23. **Four trees are planted into the square garden of side 30 m at the four corners. A rope fence is to be put around the trees. What length of rope will be required, if 2 m is required for tying the each knot?**

A) 120 m   B) 122 m   C) 118 m   D) None of these

24. **The cost of fencing a playground at ₹ 15 per meter is ₹ 2100. If the breadth of the field is 20 m, then its length is___**

A) 50 m   B) 70 m   C) 30 m   D) 40 m

25. **Lalit walks around a square garden whose side is 50 m. One day he walked around the garden 6 times. How much distance did he walk on that day?**

A) 1500 m   B) 1600 m   C) 1250 m   D) 1200 m

26. A big square is made up of 81 small squares. After removing some small square from the big square, the given figure is obtained. The length of a small square is 2 cm and its breadth is 2 cm. Find the total area of the squares removed.

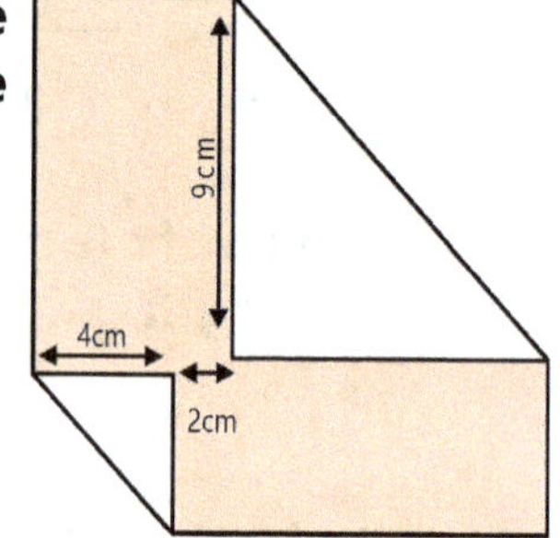

A) 81 sq. cm

B) 76 sq. cm

C) 129 sq. cm

D) 90 sq. cm

27. Two corners of a tishu paper are folded as shown. Find the area of the tishu paper when it is unfolded.

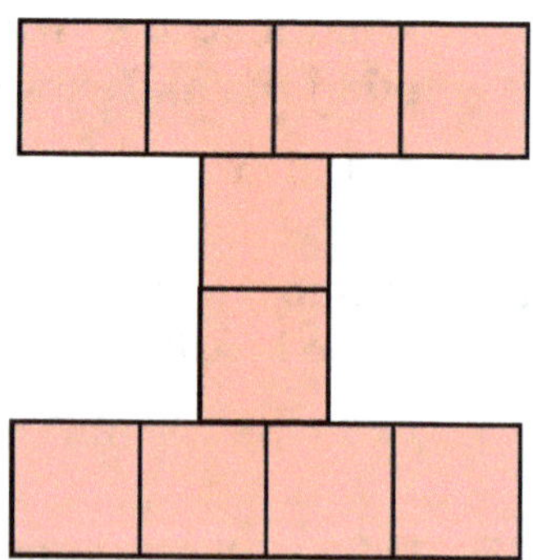

A) 49 sq. cm

B) 219 sq. cm

C) 195 sq. cm

D) 471 sq. cm

28. The given figure is made up of 10 squares of the same size. The area of the figure is 90 sq. cm. find the perimeter of the figure.

A) 54 cm

B) 15 cm

C) 48 cm

D) 32 cm

29. Which of the following figures has an area fo 15 sq. units and a perimeter of 16 units?

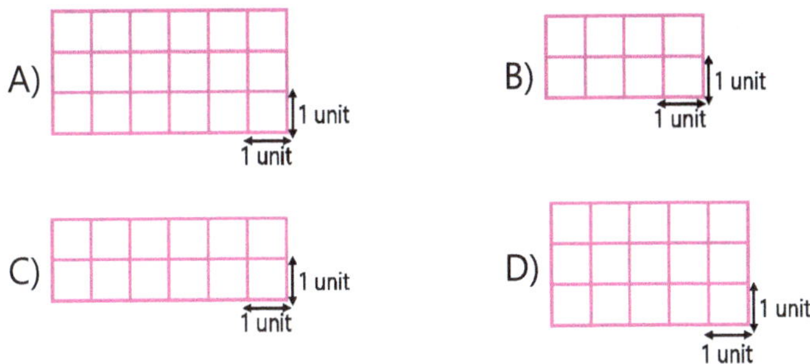

30. **The given figure shows a playground which has a rectangular tennis court with an area of 112 sq. m. Find the area of the playground that is not occupied by the tennis court.**

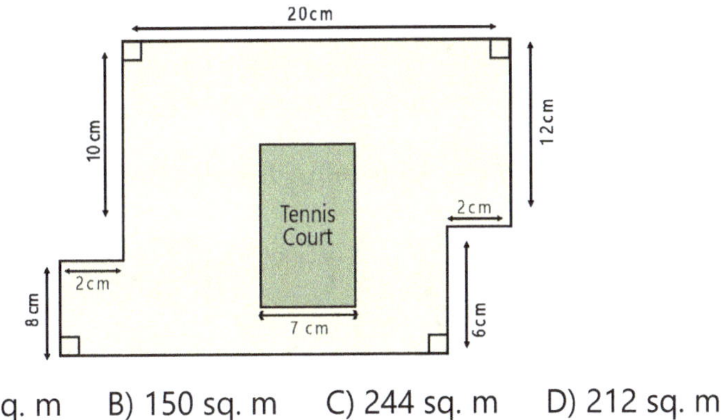

A) 400 sq. m   B) 150 sq. m   C) 244 sq. m   D) 212 sq. m

Colour your choice with color pencil				
1	2	3	4	5
A B C D	A B C D	A B C D	A B C D	A B C D
6	7	8	9	10
A B C D	A B C D	A B C D	A B C D	A B C D
11	12	13	14	15
A B C D	A B C D	A B C D	A B C D	A B C D
16	17	18	19	20
A B C D	A B C D	A B C D	A B C D	A B C D
21	22	23	24	25
A B C D	A B C D	A B C D	A B C D	A B C D
26	27	28	29	30
A B C D	A B C D	A B C D	A B C D	A B C D

MATHEMATICAL REASONING

1. How many of the following figures have line of symmetry?

A) 3   B) 5   C) 2   D) 1

2. What is the least number of squares that must be added so that the line AB becomes the line of symmetry?

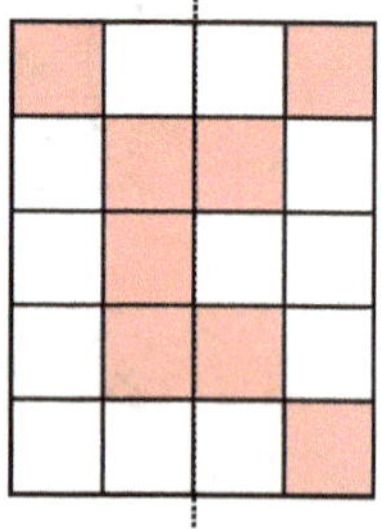

A) 5   B) 8

C) 6   D) 7

3. How many minimum numbers of squares in the figure must be shaded so that the figure becomes symmetrical along the dotted line?

A) 3   B) 2

C) 1   D) 4

4. Which of the following is a line symmetry of the given figure?

A) Only R and S

B) Only R and Q

C) Only Q

D) All P, Q, R and S

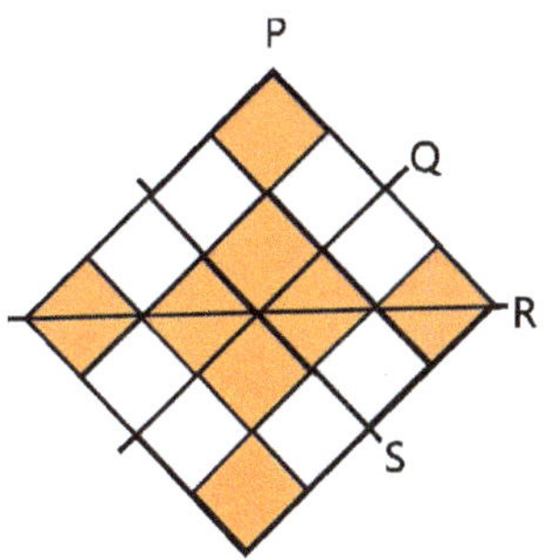

5. What is the least number of squares that must be shaded so that the figure has MN as a line of symmetry?

A) 9   B) 3

C) 5   D) 4

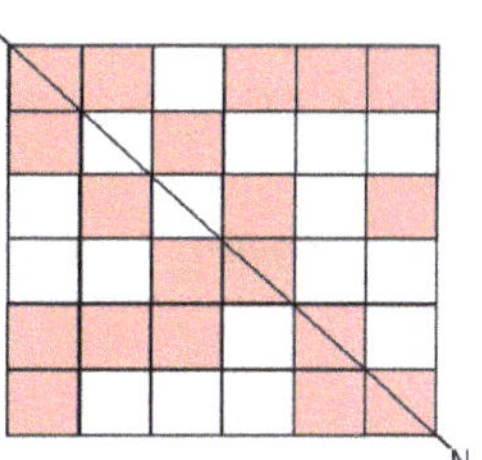

6. Which of the following options has a line of symmetry?

A) 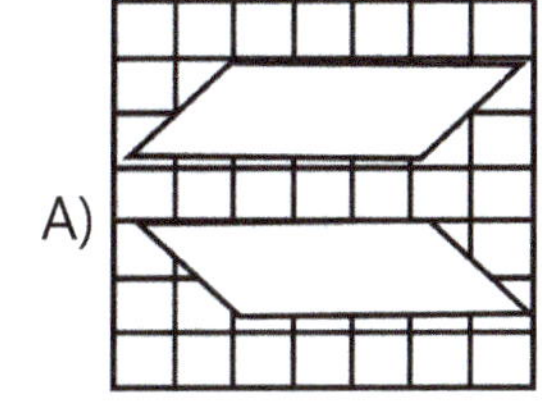

B) 

C) 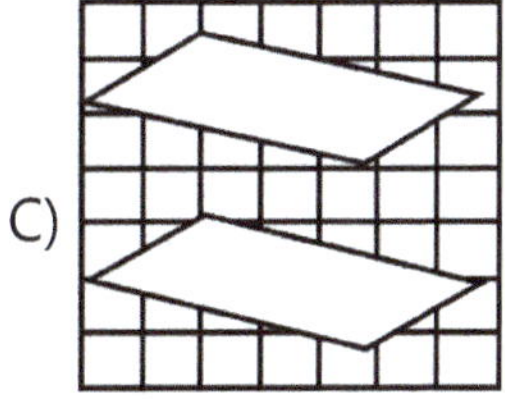

D) None of these

7. Which of the following letters have line of symmetry?

A) 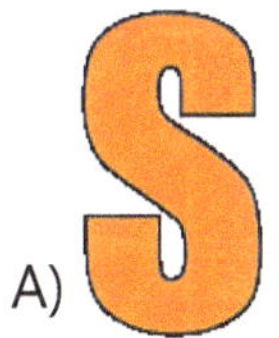 B) 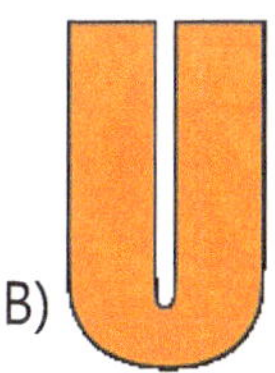 C) 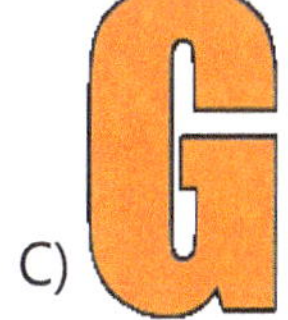 D) 

8. Which of the following figure have a line of symmetry?

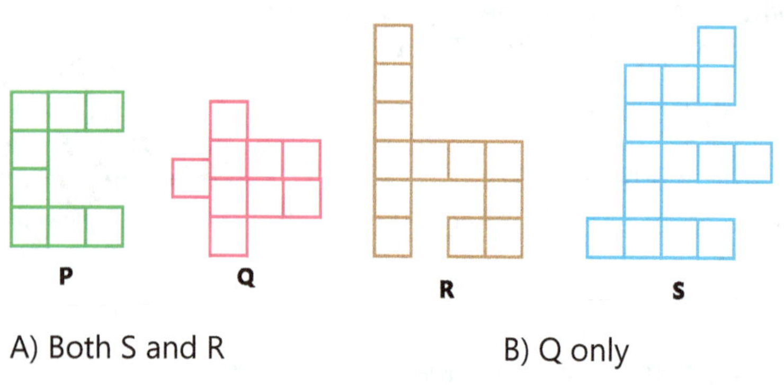

A) Both S and R

B) Q only

C) P only

D) Both P and Q

9. **Which of the following figures have a line of symmetry?**

A) 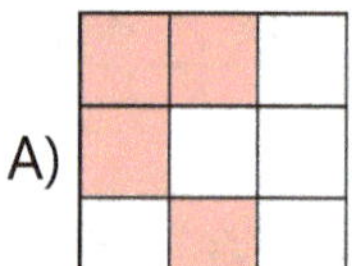 B) 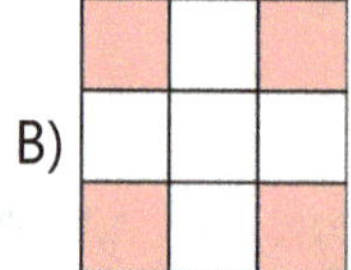 C) 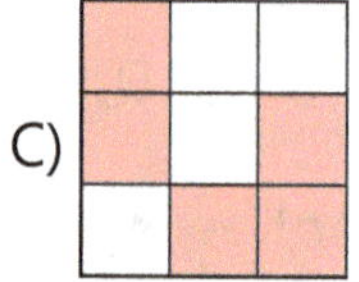 D) 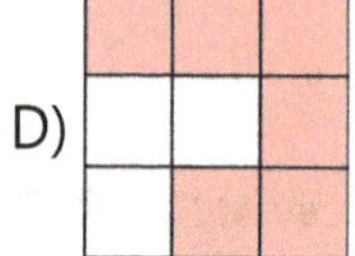

10. **How many lines of symmetry does the given figure have?**

A) 0

B) 5

C) 6

D) 4

11. **How many of the following letters have exactly two lines of symmetry?**

A) 0   B) 4   C) 8   D) 1

12. **Which square must be unshaded so that the figure has a line of symmetry?**

A) P

B) Q

C) R

D) R

13. **Which square must be unshaded so that the figure has a line of symmetry?**

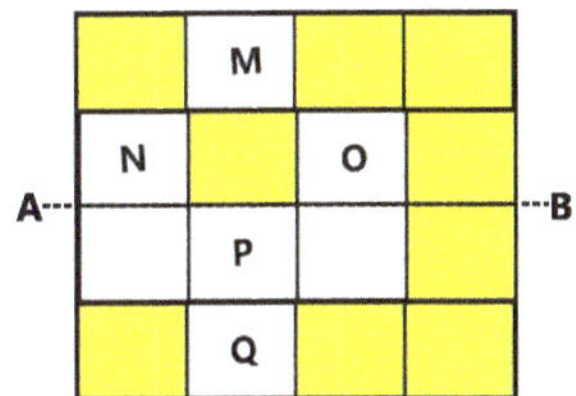

A) I
B) II
C) III
D) IV

14. **Which of the following dotted line is a line of symmetry?**

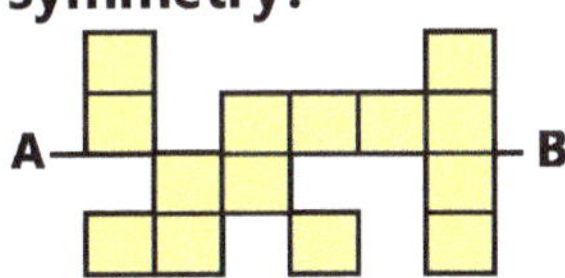

A) L
B) M
C) None of these
D) N

15. **Which of the following squares must be shaded so that the dotted line AB becomes the line of symmetry?**

A) P
B) M
C) O
D) Q

ACHIEVERS SECTION (HOTS)

16. **What is the smallest number of squares that must be added so that the line AB becomes a line of symmetry?**

A) 4
B) 9
C) 7
D) 5

17. **What is the smallest of squares that must be shaded so that the figure has a line of symmetry?**

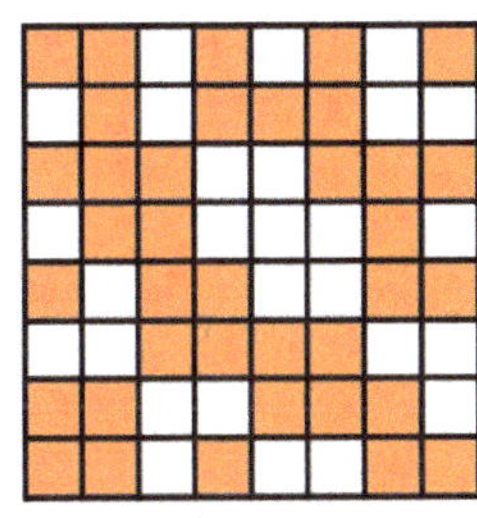

A) 2 B) 3 C) 7 D) 5

18. **What is the smallest number of squares that must be added so that the line AB becomes a line of symmetry?**

A) 4

B) 1

C) 5

D) 2

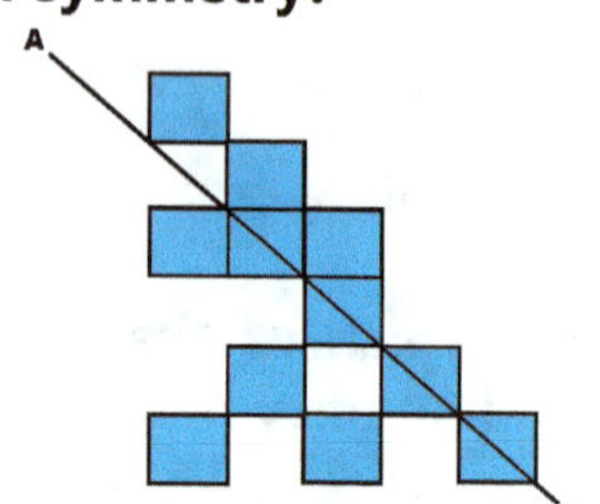

19. **How many lines of symmetry does the given figure have?**

A) 0

B) 5

C) 2

D) 1

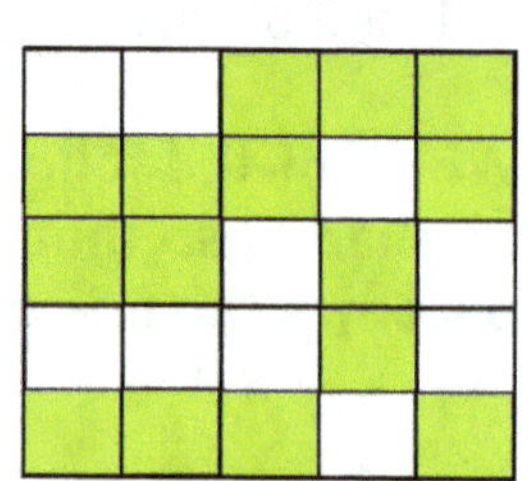

20. **The minimum number of squares that must be shaded, so that the given figure has a line of symmetry is _______.**

A) 1

B) 4

C) 0

D) 3

Colour your choice with color pencil

1	2	3	4	5
A B C D	A B C D	A B C D	A B C D	A B C D
6	**7**	**8**	**9**	**10**
A B C D	A B C D	A B C D	A B C D	A B C D
11	**12**	**13**	**14**	**15**
A B C D	A B C D	A B C D	A B C D	A B C D
16	**17**	**18**	**19**	**20**
A B C D	A B C D	A B C D	A B C D	A B C D

CHAPTER 8

DATA HANDLING

* Answer the the questions using information in given pictograph or picturegraph
* Answer the the questions using given line graphs and bar graphs

MATHEMATICAL REASONING

DIRECTION (1-3): The given bar graph shows the favorite sports of the students of class V. Study the bar carefully and answer the following questions.

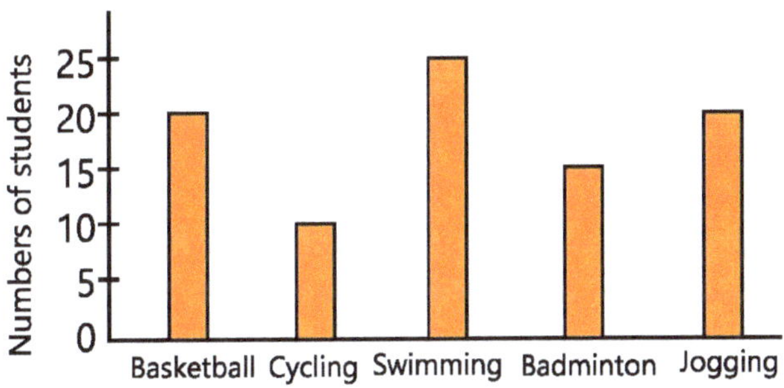

1. **Which two sports are equally liked by the students?**

   A) Basketball and Jogging

   B) Cycling and Badminton

   C) Swimming and Jogging

   D) Badminton and Swimming

2. **How many students like basketball and badminton together?**

   A) 50   B) 35   C) 45   D)70

3. **How many more students like jogging than cycling?**

   A) 35   B) 7   C) 10   D) 20

DIRECTION (4-6): The given pictograph shows the number of students of class VI participated in different competition at Annual Function.

Competition	Number of students who participated
Music	✿ ✿ ✿ ✿ ✿
Dancing	✿ ✿ ✿ ✿ ✿ ✿ ✿ ✿
Painting	✿ ✿ ✿
Art & Craft	✿ ✿ ✿ ✿ ✿ ✿ ✿ ✿ ✿
Singing	✿ ✿ ✿

Each ✿ stand for 17 students

4. **How many students took part in the music competition?**

   A) 10   B) 20   C) 85   D) 80

5. **How many students participated in the dancing competition?**

   A) 50   B) 175   C) 155   D) 136

6. **How many more students participated in art & craft than in singing and painting together?**

   A) 51   B) 95   C) 48   D) 90

DIRECTION (7-8): The line graph given below shows the number of bikes Vihan sold over the past 5 months.

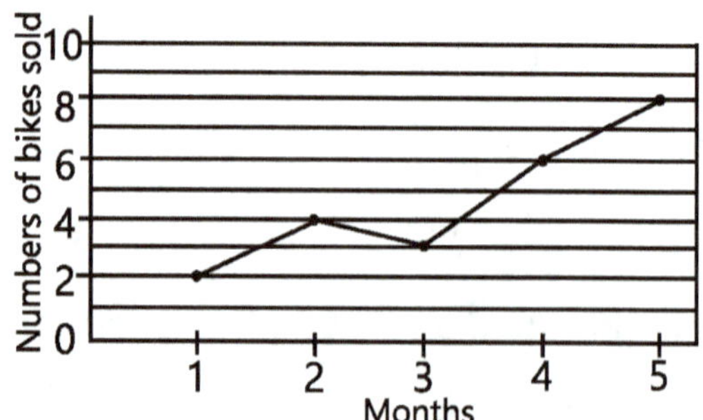

7. **How many more bikes did he sell in the last 2 months than in the first 3 months?**

A) 12   B) 4   C) 10   D) 6

8. **If Vihan got ₹ 20,000 for every bike sold, then what is the total amount he made over the past 5 months?**

A) 250000   B) 220000   C) 480000   D) 520000

DIRECTION (9-11): The given pictograph shows favourite subjects chosen by students of Class VII.

English	😊 😊 😊 😊 😊
History	😊 😊 😊 😊
Science	😊 😊
Mathematics	😊 😊 😊 😊 😊
Hindi	😊 😊 😊

Each 😊 stands for 4 students

9. **How many more students chose history as their favourite subject than hindi ?**

A) 9   B) 4   C) 14   D) 22

10. **Which subject were choose the least?**

A) History   B) Science   C) Hindi   D) English

11. **How many students are there in class-7?**

A) 80   B) 85   C) 95   D) 76

DIRECTION (12-14): The given line graph shows the number of pizzas sold on 5 consecutive days of a week. Study the line graph carefully and answer the following questions.

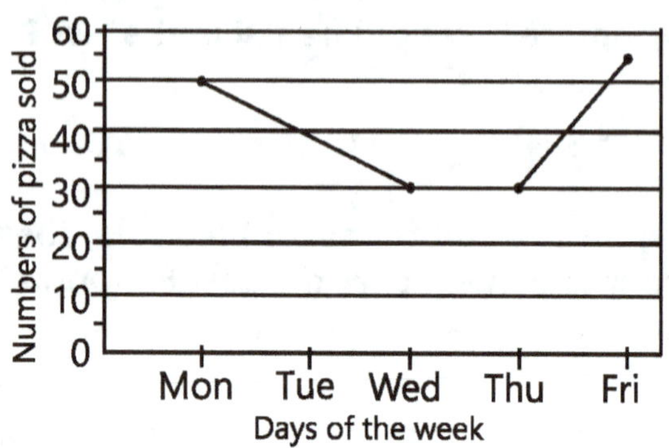

12. How many less pizzas were sold on Thursday than on Monday?

A) 55   B) 20   C) 30   D) 15

13. The differences between the greatest number of pizzas sold and the least number of pizzas sold is______.

A) 25   B) 30   C) 55   D) 45

14. If a profit of ₹ 15 was made on every pizza sold, then how much profit was made on Tuesday?

A) ₹ 350   B) ₹ 400   C) ₹ 600   D) ₹ 480

DIRECTION (15-17): The given bar graph shows the number of residents at 6 places. Study the bar graph carefully and answer the following questions.

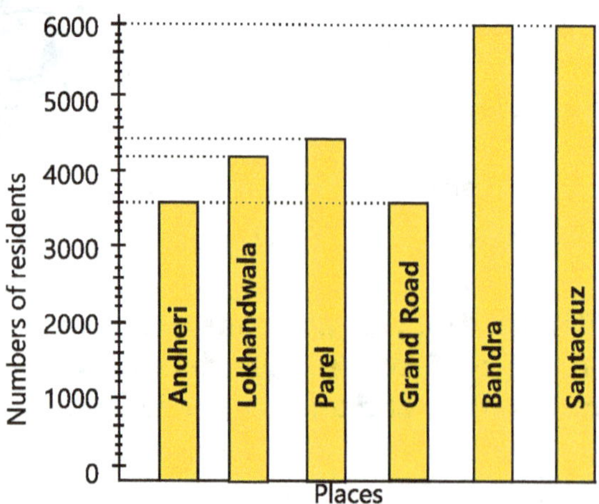

15. There were 4100 residents residing at______.

    A) Andheri   B) Lokhandwala

    C) Parel   D) Bandra

16. How many more residents were residing at Bandra than at Parel?

    A) 1600   B) 1900   C) 1500   D) 1200

17. How many residents were there altogether at the 6 places?

    A) 21000   B) 20000   C) 22500   D) 27400

DIRECTION (18-20): The given line graph shows the height of five students. Study the line graph carefully and answer the following questions.

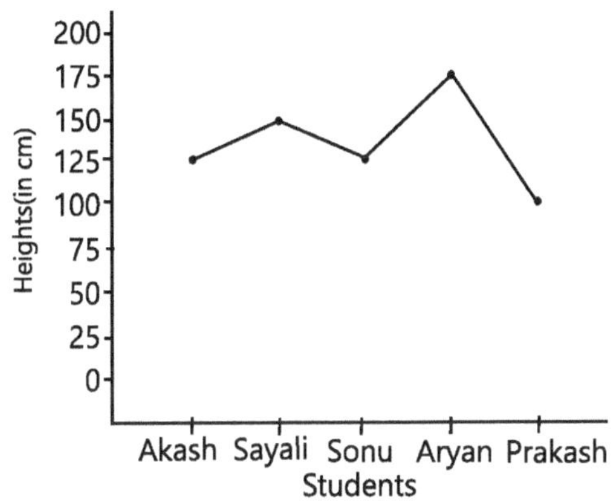

18. How many students has height less than 150 cm?

    A) 7   B) 2   C) 3   D) 5

19. Difference between the height of Sayali and Prakash is____.

    A) 50 cm   B) 70 cm   C) 85 cm   D) 20 cm

20. Which of the following students have same height?

    A) Akash, Manish   B) Sayali, Aryan

    C) Sonu, Prakash   D) Akash, Sonu

21. The given line graph shows the amount of milk used by Namish from May to September. Express the amount of milk used in August as a fraction of the total amount of milk used.

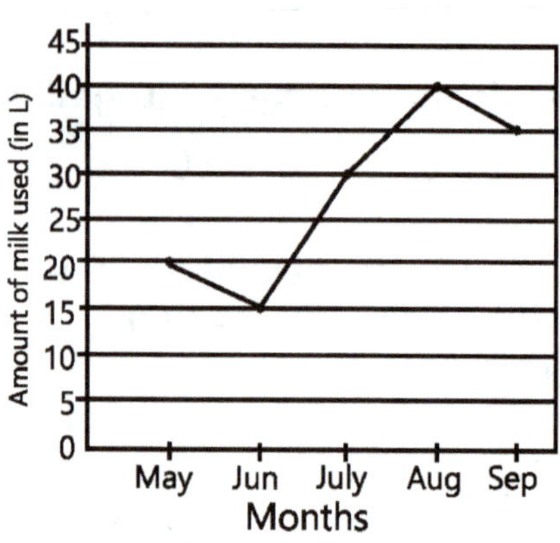

A) $\dfrac{3}{14}$ B) $\dfrac{4}{7}$ C) $\dfrac{2}{7}$ D) $\dfrac{3}{150}$

22. Four marbles P, Q, R and S are placed inside a container, one after another. The given bar graph shows the weight of the container when empty and when different marbles are placed in it. Which marble is the heaviest?

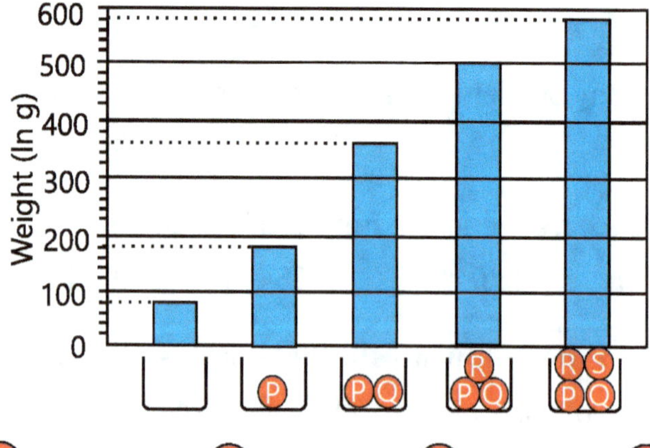

A)    B)    C)    D) 

23. **The given bar graph shows the amount of money Anjali and Gayatri saved from May to Sep.**

Who saved more amount and by how much during 5 months?

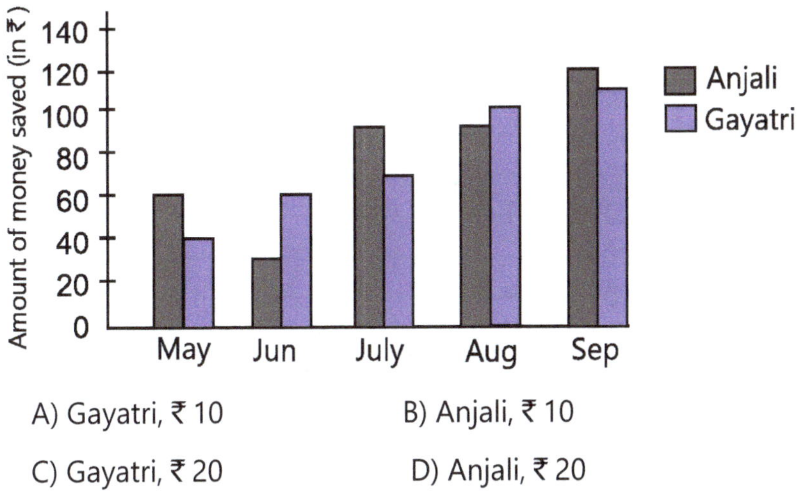

A) Gayatri, ₹ 10

B) Anjali, ₹ 10

C) Gayatri, ₹ 20

D) Anjali, ₹ 20

24. **The given bar graph shows the number of peoples in five places. Each person donated ₹ 19 to the foundation. If the total donation is ₹ 1995, then how many peoples of place D donate the money?**

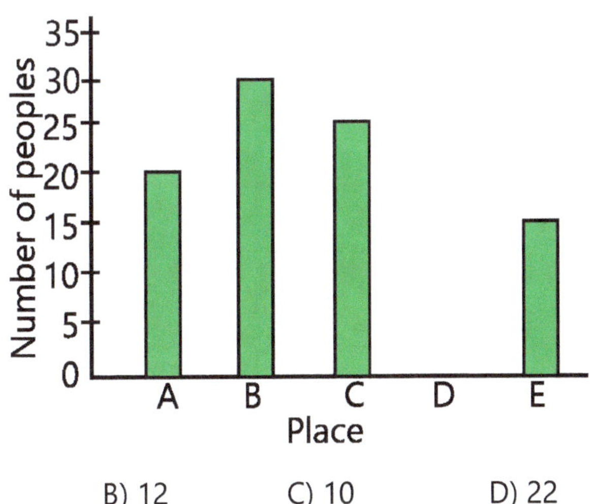

A) 15

B) 12

C) 10

D) 22

25. **The given bar graph shows the amount of money Tarun earned in a week by selling vegetables in his store.**

If he sold 12 cabbages for ₹ 6, then how many cabbages did he sold in the week?

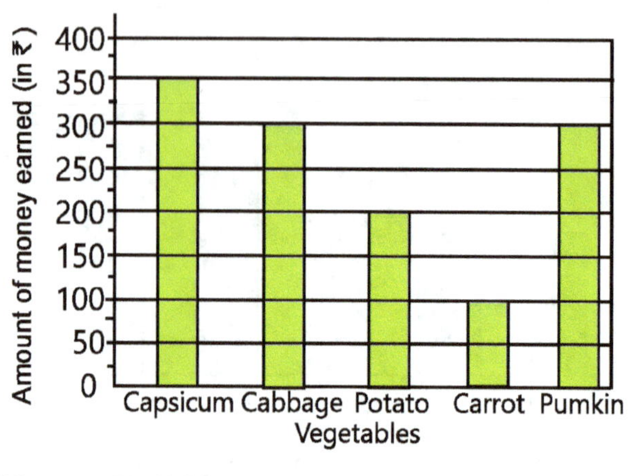

A) 1100   B) 1200   C) 1500   D) 600

Colour your choice with color pencil

1	2	3	4	5
A B C D	A B C D	A B C D	A B C D	A B C D
6	**7**	**8**	**9**	**10**
A B C D	A B C D	A B C D	A B C D	A B C D
11	**12**	**13**	**14**	**15**
A B C D	A B C D	A B C D	A B C D	A B C D
16	**17**	**18**	**19**	**20**
A B C D	A B C D	A B C D	A B C D	A B C D
21	**22**	**23**	**24**	**25**
A B C D	A B C D	A B C D	A B C D	A B C D

TOPICS COVERED:

* Patterns:(i) Number pattern (ii) Figure pattern
* Analogy Comparing two pairs of given figures or terms
* Odd One Out: Identify the odd term, figure or objest amongst given terms, figures or objects
* Counting the figures
* Embedded Figures: Identify the given figure hidden in answer figures
* Mirror Images/Water Images
* Direction Sense Test
* Alphabet Test
* Ranking Test: Finding the position of term or object from given position
* Simple puzzles
* Simple sitting arrangments
* Coding-Decoding
* Simple Blood Relations
* Day and Dates & Possible Combinations

MATHEMATICAL REASONING

1. **In a line of girls, Nitu is 10th from the top and Sonali is 5th from the bottom. If Nitu is 5 students ahead of Sonali, then how many students are there in the line?**

   A) 15   B) 20   C) 21   D) None of these

2. **Which of the given options will complete the given pattern?**

   4C, 10E, ?, 22I, 28K

   A) 4 C   B) 22 I   C)16 G   D) 10 E

3. **Which of the following options is the correct mirror image of Fig. (X)?**

A) 

B) 

C) 

D) 

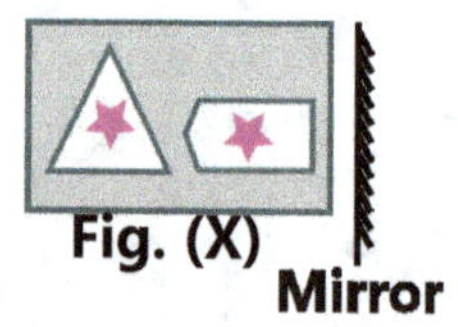

Fig. (X)

Mirror

4. **Madhav is older than Rohan. Dinesh is younger than Rohan and Neeraj. Neeraj is not as old as Madhav, Who is the eldest amongst all?**

A) Madhav

B) Rohan

C) Madhav or Rohan

D) Data inadequate

5. **Which of the following figures will complete the pattern in Fig. (X)?**

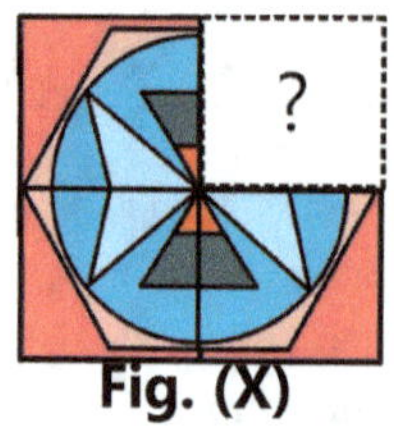

Fig. (X)

A) 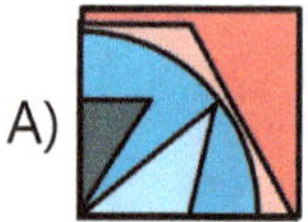

B) 

C) 

D) 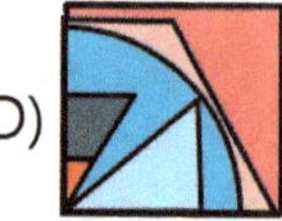

6. **Five boys are standing in the garden facing North. Mahesh is to the left of Kabir and to the right of Pranav. Raj is to the right of Kabir. Girish is between Kabir and Raj. Who is second from the right end?**

A) Raj

B) Kabir

C) Girish

D) Mahesh

7. **Count the number of squares in the given figure**

A) 15

B) 11

C) 9

D) 14

8. **There is a certain relationship between figures A and B. Establish the similar relationship between figures C and D by selecting suitable figure from the options which will replace the (?) in figure S.**

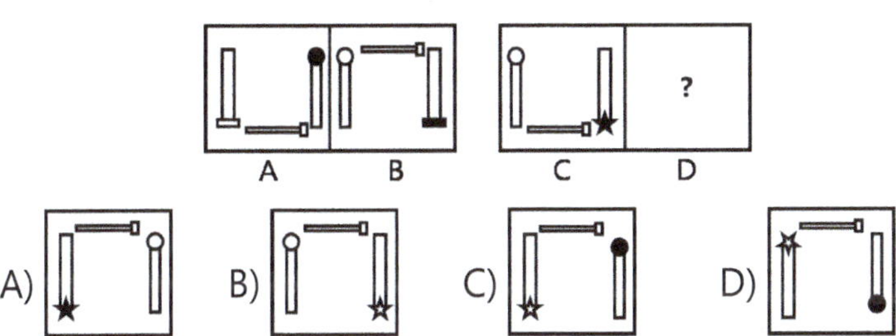

9.. **Select the correct water image of the given combination of letters.**

MANGO

A) MANGO (water image)   B) OGNAM   C) MANGO   D) NGOAM

10. **Namit correctly remembers that he visited Goa before thirteen of May but after ninth of May. His mother correctly remembers that Namit visited Goa after eleventh of May but before fourteenth of May. On which date of May did Namit visit Goa?**

   A) 10th   B) 12th   C) 13th   D) 11th

11. **The model of a tower shown here in made up of unit boxes stacked on top of each other. How many unit boxes in all are used to form the tower?**

   A) 30   B) 28

   C) 39   D) 44

12. **How many different possible combinations of one Juices and one snacks can be formed from the given chocolate and toys?**

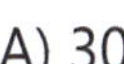

A) 20   B) 18   C) 27   D) 14

13. Arrange the following in a meaningful order

1.City   2. World   3. Country

4. Village   5. State

A) 4, 3, 2, 5, 1   B) 4, 1, 5, 3, 2

C) 2, 5, 3, 4, 1   D) 1, 2, 4, 5, 3

14. Divya is facing the Hospital. What will she be facing, if she turns $\frac{4}{7}$ clockwise?

A) College   B) Temple

C) Bank   D) Library

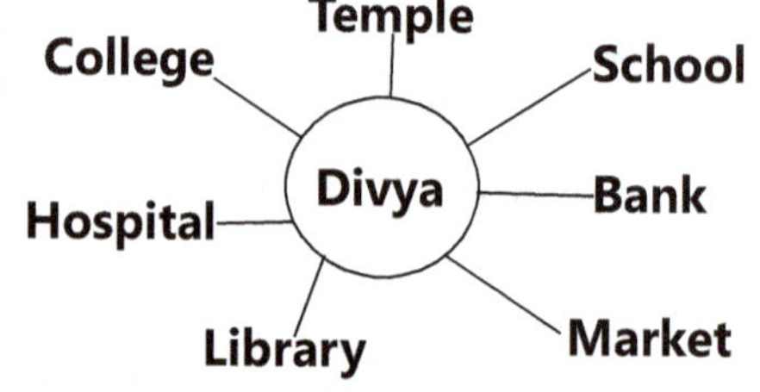

15. Find the missing number, if same rule is followed in all the three figures.

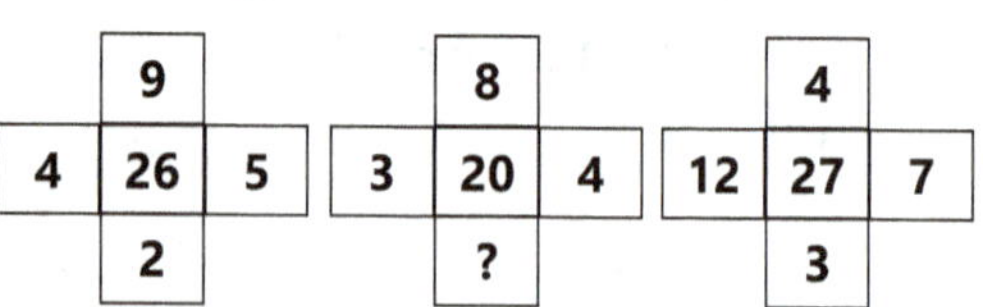

A) 9   B) 12

C) 8   D) 11

16. Which of the following options will continue the same series as established by the problem figures?

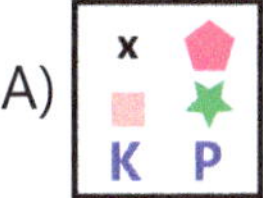 A)
 B)
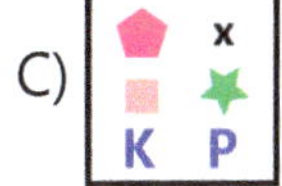 C)
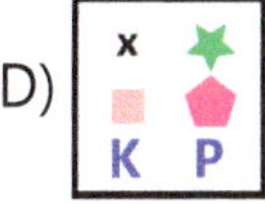 D)

17. **Find the missing number, if a certain rule is followed either row-wise or column-wise.**

   A) 70

   B) 42

   C) 55

   D) 30

5	60	4
2	?	7
3	72	8

18. **Select the odd one out.**

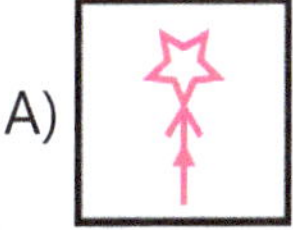 A)
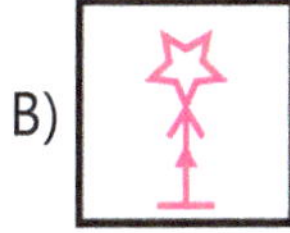 B)
 C)
 D)

19. **If the first and sixth letters in the word 'POPULATION' were interchanged, also the second and seventh letters are interchanged and so on, then which letter will be the nineth from the right end in the new arrangement?**

   A) L   B) T   C) N   D) O

20. **Select a figure from the options which will continue the same as series as established by the problem figures.**

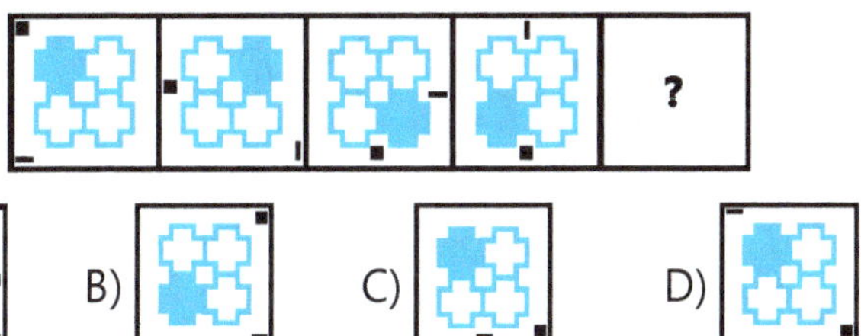

21. **Tushar is facing the market. If he turns 135° in anti-clock wise direction, then what will he be facing finally?**

A) Hospital   B) College   C) Garden   D) Shopping mall

22. **Which of the following options best depicts the relationship amongst, Girls, Teachers, Nurses?**

 A)
 B)
 C)
D)

23. **Which of the following options will complete the pattern in Fig.(X)?**

A) 

B) 

C) 

D) 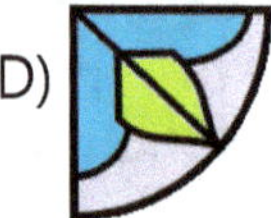

Fig.(X)

24. **Select a figure from the options in which Fig (X) is exactly embedded as one of its parts.**

A) 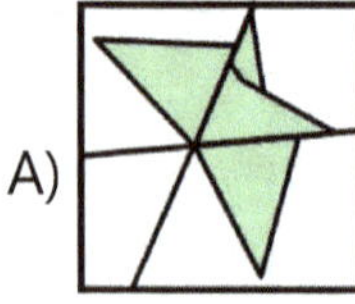

B) 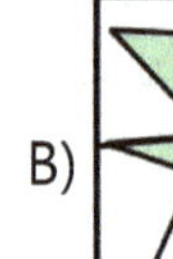

C) 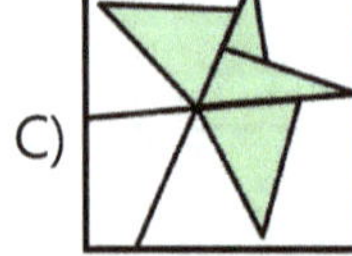

D) 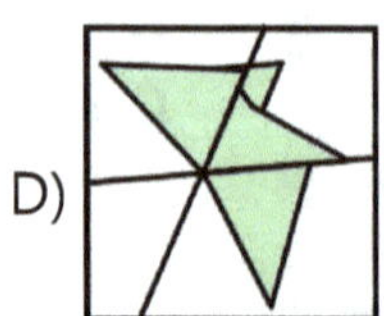

Fig.(X)

25. **If in a certain code language, NORMAL is written as OPSNBI, then how will DIFFICULT be written in that language?**

A) VIGGJEIU

B) JEVIJGGU

C) EJOOJVIU

D) EJGGJDVMU

26. **How many minimum numbers of parallel lines are required to make the given figure?**

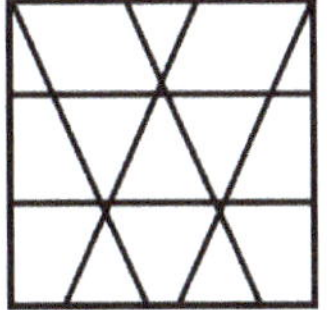

A) 9

B) 10

C) 14

D) 7

27. **Naman's school holidays starts is on fourth day after third Sunday of May 20XX. On which date will Naman's holiday start?**

May 20XX						
Mon	Tue	Wed	Thu	Fri	Sat	Sun
			1	2	3	4
5	6	7	8	9	10	11
12	13	14	15	16	17	18
19	20	21	22	23	24	25
26	27	28	29	30	31	

A) May 15　　　B) May 22　　　C) May 18　　　D) May 4

28. **Find the correct water image of the given Fig. (X).**

A) 

B) 

Fig. (X)

C) 

D) 

29. **In the given Venn diagram, the girls who are actors and are models are indicated by which number?**

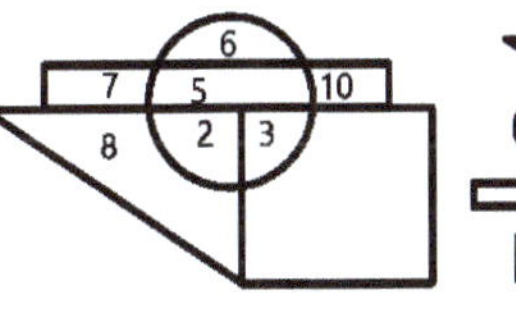

A) 8   B) 2   C) 1   D) 5

30. In a certain code language 'earth' is called 'sky', 'sky' is called 'water' and 'water' is called 'light', then if someone is thirsty what would he drink?

A) Sky   B) Water   C) Earth   D) Light

Colour your choice with color pencil

1	2	3	4	5
A B C D	A B C D	A B C D	A B C D	A B C D
6	**7**	**8**	**9**	**10**
A B C D	A B C D	A B C D	A B C D	A B C D
11	**12**	**13**	**14**	**15**
A B C D	A B C D	A B C D	A B C D	A B C D
16	**17**	**18**	**19**	**20**
A B C D	A B C D	A B C D	A B C D	A B C D
21	**22**	**23**	**24**	**25**
A B C D	A B C D	A B C D	A B C D	A B C D
26	**27**	**28**	**29**	**30**
A B C D	A B C D	A B C D	A B C D	A B C D

Hints & Explanations

1 Number Sense

1. (C) : Two hundred three thousand, five hundred twenty three is written as 203,523

2. (D) :

3. (B) : Greatest four-digit number 9999. Now 9999 = 9000 + 900 + 90 + 9 IXCMXCIX.

4. (B) :

5. (B) : Place value of 6 at ten thousand place 60000

Place value of 6 at tense place = 60

And 60000 = 60 × 1000

6. (C) : (A) XL = 40 (B) XC = 90

(C) LT is meaningless

(D) LX = 60

7. (A) :

8. (A) : DCCC = 800, LXXX = 80 And, 800 > 80

9. (B) : 115 = 100 + 10 + 5 = CXV

10. (A) : The largest 4 digit number is 9999

∴ Required difference = 9999 + 1 = 10000

11. (A) : 10 Lakh = 1000000 = 1 million

12. (B) : The successor of 424520 = 424520 + 1 = 424521

13. (A) :

14. (A) : Place value of 5 In 42,352,160 = 50000

Place value 8 in 24,68 962 = 8000

∴ Required difference = 50000 − 8000

= 42000

15. (D) : Smallest 5-digit number = 10000

∴ Predecessor of = 10000 − 1 = 9999

16. (B) : 9,22,320 < 9,23,420 < 9,23,878 < 9,24,520

17. (A) : Face value of 5 in 3,11, 528 is i.e., five

18. (C) : (A) 4,85,932 when rounded off to nearest thousands becomes 486000

(B) 4,80,508 when rounded off to nearest thousands becomes 4,81,000

(C) 4,86,702 when rounded off to nearest thousands becomes 4,87,000

(D) 4,85,302 when rounded off to nearest thousands becomes 4,85,000

So, 4,86,702 is greatest

when rounded off to nearest thousands.

19. (C) :

20. (B) : The smallest 4-digit number that can be formed using digits 5, 3, 1 and 7 each atleast ones is 1357

21. (A) : Height of Pole P = DXXX = 530 cm

    Height of Pole Q = DL = 550 cm

    As, 530<550

    So, Pole P is shorter.

22. (C) : DCLXV = 500 + 100 + 50 + 10 + 5 = 665

23. (D) : According to given information, the 6-digits number is even.

    ∴ 6th digit will be either 3, 4, 2, 1, 5, 7

    So, the smallest 6-digit even number that can be formed is 123456

24. (B) : Fifty two crore twelve lakh sixty six thousand twenty two is written in numerals as 52,12,66,022.

25. (C) : 647941 is the greatest number among all the numbers.

    So, auditorium C is the greatest number of seats.

26. (A) : Jyoti's number = MCLXX = 1000 + 100 + 70 = 1170

    Now, Swapna's number = Successor of 1170 = 1171

And Akshaya's number = Predecessor of 1170 = 1169

27. (B) : Place value 6 in 6590324 is 6000000.

28. (D) :

29. (A) : (A) 1350 = 1000 + 300 + 50

    = MCCLL (Incorrect)

    (B) 1400 = 1000 + 400

    = MCD (correct)

    (C) 1051 = 1000 + 50 +1

    =MLI (Correct)

    (D) 1100 = 1000 + 100

    = MC (Correct)

30. (B) : (P) Eighty four lakh seventy one thousand four hundred seventy one is written as 84,71,471

    (Q) Thirty two lakh fourty two thousand four hundred ninety nine is written as 32,42,499

    (R) Fourteen lakh twenty one thousand four hundred ninety eight is written as 14,21,498

    (S) Seventy nine lakh fourty eight thousand eight hundred eighty is written as 79,48,880

1. (D) : CMMXXIX + CMXII

   = 929 + 912 = 9841 =

MDCCCXLI

2. (B) : We have 1 fathom = 6 feet

1 feet = $\dfrac{1}{6}$ fathom

Submarine was lacated underwater at 240 feet.

∴ Location of ship underwater in fathoms = 240 ÷ 6

3. (B) : Statement 1 is false , as L cannot be substracted V and X.

4. (C) :

5. (A) : DCLXX – CDLV = 670 – 455 = 215

CCLX + LXXX = 260 + 80 = 340

215 < 340 and CCXV < CCCXL

6. (A) : Total number of tiles produced = 890043

Number of good quality = 885178

∴ Number of tiles which were defective

= 890043 – 885178 = 4865

7. (B) : 675432 – 45 = 675387

And 675387 X 12 = 8104644

8. (B) : Total numbers of sharpners produced

=1027404 + 342468 = 1369872

So, numbers of sharpners packed in 63 boxes = 1369872

∴ Numbers of sharpners packed in 1 boxes

= 1369872 ÷ 63 = 21744

9. (B) : 8th multiple of 9 = 9 × 8 = 72

12th multiple of 9 = 9 × 12 =108

Now, ☺ =2 ×(108 – 72) = 2 × 36 = 72

10. (D) : We have, 2 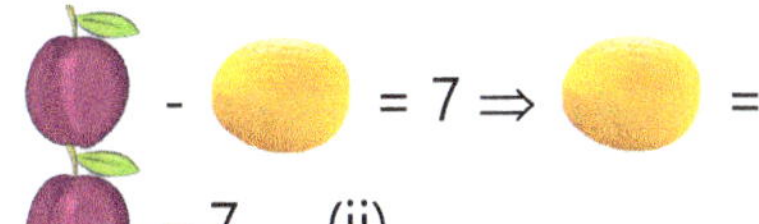 = 136 .....(i)

 = 7 ⇒ = – 7......(ii)

Putting the value of (ii) in (i), we get

2 (-7) + =136

⇒ 2 – 14 + = 136

⇒ 3 = 136 + 14

⇒ = $\dfrac{150}{3}$ = 50

11. (D) : Let x be the required number.

So, 1 lakh – x = 75413

⇒ 100000 – x = 75413

⇒ x = 100000 – 75413 = 24587

12. (C) : 15 × 6 + 48 ÷ 6 + 14 = 15 × 6 + 8 + 14

=90 + 8 + 14 =112

13. (A) :

	84			144
2	84	2	2	144
2	42	6	6	72
3	21	6	6	12
7	7	2	2	2
	1			1

∴ H.C.F. = 2 x 6 = 12

14. (B) : Factors of 20 are 1, 2, 4, 5, 10, 20

∴ Prime factors of 20 are, 2 and 5

15. (B) : We have,

425622 + 159912 = 585534

Rounding off the result to the nearest hundreds, we get 585500

16. (A) : Total numbers of chairs = 588

Number of departments = 14

∴ Numbers of chairs in each department

$= \dfrac{588}{14} = 42$

17. (D) : 2nd multiple of 2 = 2 × 2 = 4

And 8th multiple of 8 = 8 × 8 = 64

∴ Required sum = 4 + 64 = 68

From the given option, 68 is divisible by 2

18. (B) : (A) Age of Akshay = 5A years

(B) Age of Tina = (5 - A) years

(C) Age of Om = 5A years

(D) Age of Gayatri = (A + 5) years

19. (B) : 5467812 ÷ 28 = 195279

20. (A) : Total numbers of cloths sale in all three years

=214532 + 12675 + 319067 = 546274

21. (B) : Total number of peoples working = 9089752

Number of people work in Tata company and Indira company

= 1478123 + 1878543 = 5235209

∴ Number of peoples work in Durga Company = 9089752 − 5235209 = 3854543

22. (B) : Total number of boxes = 5412

Number of toys in each box = 57

∴ Total number of toys store in godown = 5412 x 57 = 308484

23. (D) : Total earning = ₹ 4789000

Total expenses = ₹ 276894

∴ Total savings = ₹ (4789000 − 276894) = ₹ 4512106

24. (D) : Total number of bricks = 6785431

Number of chambers = 17

So, number of bricks used for each chamber

= 6785431 ÷ 17 = 399143

25. (C) : Number of windows on

1st floor = 20

Number of floors in 1 building = 12

∴ Number of windows in 1 building

= 20 × 12 = 240

Number of buildings in the complex = 25

∴ Number of Windows in the complex

= 240 x 25 = 6000

26. (D) : P = 6, Q = 5, R = 7, S = 8

Hence, P – Q + R + S

= 6 – 5 + 7 + 8

= 1 + 15 = 16

27. (C): Total number of chairs used = 18816

Number of chairs used in 1 department

= 2 × 84 + 1 × 64 + 2 × 52

= 168 + 64 + 104 = 336

So, number of department in the building

= 18816 ÷ 336 = 56

28. (D) : Number of packet of snacks produced by company P in 1 day 8200

∴ Number of packet of snacks produced by company Q in 1 day = 8200 + 135 = 8335

So, number of packet of snacks produced by both companies P and Q in 1 day

= 8200 + 8335 = 16535

∴ Number of packet of snacks produced by both companies in 7 days = 16535 × 7 = 115745

Now, number of packet of snacks in 1 pack = 35

So, total numbers of packet of snacks formed

= 115745 ÷ 35 = 3305

29. (D): Amount of money in the account on 1st Jun = ₹ 45830

Total amount of money deposited

= ₹ (2130 + 22280) = ₹ 24410

Amount money withdrawn = ₹ 58630

∴ Balance left at the end of the month

= ₹ (45830 + 24410) = ₹ 70240

= ₹ (70240 – 58630) = ₹ 11610

30. (A) : From the given matrix, we have

A. 15430 + 8670 = 24140

B. 15470 + 12890 = 28760

C. 6790 + 8670 = 15460

and D. 6790 + 12890 = 19680

Now A + B = 24140 + 28760 = 52900

C + D = 15460 + 19680

= 35140

∴ (A + B) – (C + D)

= 52900 – 35140 = 17760

3. Fractions and Decimals

1. **(A) :** In fig. (i).

   Total numbers of equal parts = 10

   Numbers of shaded part = 3

   $\therefore$ Shaded fraction = $\frac{3}{10}$

   In fig. (i).

   Total number of equal parts = 8

   Number of shaded parts 3

   $\therefore$ Shaded fraction = $\frac{3}{8}$

   Now sum of shaded fractions

   $= \frac{3}{10} + \frac{3}{8}$

   $= \frac{12 + 15}{40} = \frac{27}{40}$

2. **(B) :** $48.77 \times 6 = 292.62$ is 0.60

   Place value of 6 in 292.62 is 0.60

3. **(A) :** Total amount of money Hema distributed = 54.39

   Amount of money distributed among six cousins = ₹ 37.72

   So, amount money Hema gave to her sixth cousin = $54.39 - 37.72 = ₹ 16.67$

4. **(D) :**

5. **(B) :**

6. **(C) :** Aryan jumped $4\frac{7}{12}$ feet i.e. $\frac{55}{12}$ feet

   Ram jumped $3\frac{1}{6}$ feet i.e. $\frac{19}{6}$ feet

   $\therefore$ Differences = $\frac{55}{12} - \frac{19}{6}$

   $= \frac{55 - 38}{12}$

   $= \frac{17}{12} = 1\frac{5}{12}$ feet

   So, Aryan jump $1\frac{5}{12}$ feet farther than Ram.

7. **(D) :** 4 tens and 10 hundredths

   $= 4 \times 10 + \frac{10}{100}$

   $= 40 + 0.10 = 40.1$

   60 tens and 8 tenths = $60 \times 10 + \frac{8}{10}$

   $= 600 + 0.8 = 600.8$

   $\therefore$ Required sum = $40.1 + 600.8 = 640.9$

8. **(A) :** Fraction of cake given to 1 friend = $\frac{1}{6}$

   Fraction of cake given to 4 friend $= 4 \times \frac{1}{6} = \frac{4}{6}$

   Fraction of cake left with Minal = $1 - \frac{4}{6} = \frac{2}{6}$

9. **(C) :** $482.20 + 726.44 = 1208.64$

   On rounding off 1208.64 to nearest tenths, we get 1208.6

10. **(D) :** So, X = 4.15

11. After rearranging the figure, we get

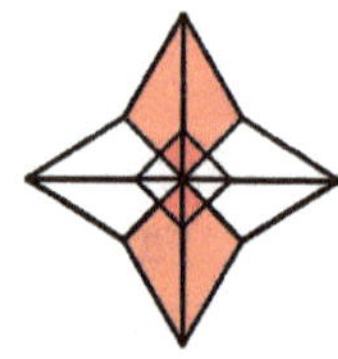

Total numbers of equal parts

= 8

Number of shaded parts = 4

∴ shaded fraction = $\dfrac{4}{8}$ = $\dfrac{1}{2}$

12. (B) : (A) $\dfrac{8}{12} = \dfrac{8 \div 4}{12 \div 4} = \dfrac{2}{3} \neq \dfrac{4}{7}$

(B) $\dfrac{8}{16} = \dfrac{8 \div 4}{16 \div 4} = \dfrac{2}{4}$

(C) $\dfrac{12}{24} = \dfrac{12 \div 12}{24 \div 12} = \dfrac{1}{2} \neq \dfrac{4}{7}$

(D) $\dfrac{24}{40} = \dfrac{24 \div 8}{40 \div 8} = \dfrac{3}{5} \neq \dfrac{4}{7}$

13. (C) : Total number of equal shapes = 25

Unshaded fraction = $\dfrac{2}{5}$

∴ Shaded fraction = $1 - \dfrac{2}{5}$ = $\dfrac{3}{5}$

Now, number of shapes to be shaded = $\dfrac{3}{5} \times 25 = 15$

14. (D) : Let the number be x.

According to question, we have

$(x - 2.9) \times 3 + 0.5 = 10.5$

$\Rightarrow 3 \times (x - 2.9) = 10.35$

$\Rightarrow x - 2.9 = 3.45$

$\Rightarrow x = 6.35$

15. (A) : Let x be the required fraction.

So, $2\dfrac{2}{5} + x 3\dfrac{3}{10}$

$\Rightarrow \dfrac{12}{5} + x = \dfrac{33}{10}$

$\Rightarrow x = \dfrac{33}{10} - \dfrac{12}{5} = \dfrac{33-24}{10} = \dfrac{9}{10}$

16. (D) : First convert to given fractions into like fractions.

L.C.M of 2, 3, 6 = 6

So, $\dfrac{1}{2} = \dfrac{1 \times 3}{2 \times 3} = \dfrac{3}{6}$; $\dfrac{2}{3} = \dfrac{2 \times 2}{3 \times 2} = \dfrac{4}{6}$; $\dfrac{2}{6} = \dfrac{2 \times 1}{6 \times 1} = \dfrac{2}{6}$

So, ascending order is,

$\dfrac{2}{6}, \dfrac{3}{6}, \dfrac{4}{6}$ i.e. $\dfrac{2}{6}, \dfrac{1}{2}, \dfrac{2}{3}$

17. (C) : Using distributive property, we have

$0.25 \times 12 = 0.25 \times (3 + 3 + 6)$

$\Rightarrow 0.25 \times 12 = 0.25 \times 3 + 0.25 \times 3 + 0.25 \times 6$

18. (B) : Let the missing number be x.

Then we have,

$0.25 + 9 + 1\dfrac{1}{8} - (6.5 \times 0.2) = x \times \dfrac{1}{4}$

$\Rightarrow 2.25 + 9 + \dfrac{9}{8} - 1.3 = x \times \dfrac{1}{4}$

$\Rightarrow 0.25 + 1.125 - 1.3 = x \times \dfrac{1}{4}$

$\Rightarrow 0.075 = x \times \dfrac{1}{4} \Rightarrow x = 0.075 \times 4$

$\Rightarrow x = 0.3$

19. (A) : Difference between 98 tenths and 580 hundrenths = $9.8 - 5.80 = 4$

Now, $24.28 \div 4 = 6.07$

20. (B) :

21. (C) : Time taken by Aisha to walk to the garden = $\dfrac{1}{8}$

hour

Time taken by Aisha to walk from garden to home $= \dfrac{1}{4}$ hour

$\therefore$ Total time taken $= \dfrac{1}{8} + \dfrac{1}{4}$

$= \dfrac{1+3}{8} = \dfrac{4}{8} = \dfrac{1}{2}$ hour

22. (C) : Weight of rice in 1 bag $= \dfrac{3}{4}$ kg

$\therefore$ Weight of rice in 42 bags

$(\dfrac{3}{4} \times 42)$ kg $= \dfrac{63}{2}$ kg $= 31.5$ kg

23. (A) : We are given that,

Amount of money Diya spent

$= \dfrac{1}{5}$ of amount of money Deepa spent

Also, amount of money Diya and Deepa spent together $= ₹216$

$\Rightarrow \dfrac{1}{5}$ amount of money Deepa spent + amount of money Deepa spent $= ₹216$

$\Rightarrow (\dfrac{1}{5} + 1)$ of amount of money Deepa spent $= ₹216$

$\Rightarrow \dfrac{6}{5} \times$ amount of money Deepa spent $= ₹216$

$\Rightarrow$ Amount of money Deepa spent $= ₹(216 \times \dfrac{5}{6}) = ₹180$

So, amount of money Diya spent $= ₹(\dfrac{1}{5} \times 180) = ₹36$

Now, amount of money Ragini and Diya spent together $= ₹95$

$\Rightarrow$ Amount of money Ragini spent $= ₹(95 - 36) = ₹59$

24. (B) : $24.22 \times 4 = 96.88$

$2.422 \times 4 = 9.688$

Required difference

$96.88 - 9.688 = 87.192$

25. (A) : Time spent by Amruta in a week

$= 7\dfrac{1}{2}$ hours $= \dfrac{15}{2}$ hours

Time spend by Amruta on each day $1\dfrac{1}{2}$ hours

$= \dfrac{3}{2}$ hours

So, number of days she practice in a week

$\dfrac{15}{2} + \dfrac{3}{2} = \dfrac{15}{2} \times \dfrac{2}{3} = 5$

26. (A) : We have,

$$\dfrac{2\dfrac{5}{4} - 5\dfrac{1}{6} + 3\dfrac{1}{3}}{0.087 + 0.3717 + 0.9}$$

$$= \dfrac{\dfrac{13}{4} - \dfrac{31}{6} + \dfrac{10}{3}}{0.087 + 0.413} = \dfrac{\dfrac{39 - 62 + 40}{12}}{0.5}$$

$$= \dfrac{\dfrac{17}{12}}{0.5} = \dfrac{17}{6} = 2.833$$

27. (A) : The value of $(30.5 - 30.4)$ $+ (30.3 - 30.2) + (30.1 - 30.0)$ $+ (29.9 - 29.8) + (29.7 - 29.6)$ $+ (29.5 - 29.4) + (29.3 - 29.2)$ $+ (29.1 - 29.0)$

$= 0.1 + 0.1 + 0.1 + 0.1 + 0.1$ $+ 0.1 + 0.1 + 0.1 = 0.8$

28. (D) : Shaded fraction of first figure is,

$$P = 1 + \frac{6}{10} = \frac{16}{10} = \frac{8}{5} 1 \frac{3}{5}$$

In decimal form, Q = 1.6

Shaded fraction of second figure is,

$$R = 1 + 1 + 1 + \frac{5}{10} = 3 + \frac{1}{2}$$

$$= \frac{7}{2} = 3 \frac{1}{3}$$

In decimal form, S = 3.5

29. (A) : (A) $\frac{3}{6} = \frac{3 \div 3}{6 \div 3} = \frac{1}{2}$

(B) $\frac{1}{100}$ if 1 cm = $\frac{1}{100} \times 10$ mm

$= \frac{1}{10}$ mm

(C) $\frac{1}{2}$ of hour = $\frac{1}{2} \times 60$ minutes

(D) $\frac{5}{6} = 0.8333$, $\frac{6}{5} = 1.2$

$\therefore \frac{5}{6} \neq \frac{6}{5}$

30. (C) : We have,

P = 231.22 + 7.4 = 238.62

Q = 18.65 - 6.32 = 12.33

R = 871.09 - 396.02 = 475.07

So, R - P + Q

= 475.07 - 238.62 + 12.33

= 248.78

4. Measurements

1. (D) : Weight of 5 cups of wheat = 690 g

$\therefore$ Weight of 1 cup of wheat

= (690 ÷ 5)g = 130 g

Weight of 1 glass of wheat = 200 g

$\therefore$ Required difference = (200 − 138)g = 62 g

2. (C) : Required time is 3 hrs 40 mins before 6 : 20 p.m. i. e.: 2 : 40 p.m

3. (C) : $5 \frac{2}{3}$ hrs = $\frac{17}{3}$ hrs

1 hr = 60 mins

$\therefore \frac{17}{3}$ hrs = $\frac{17}{3} \times 60$ mins

= 340 mins

4. (A) : Let quantity of water on pool Q be x litres.

$\therefore$ Quantity of water in pool P = 5x litres

Total water in both of pools = x + 5x = 90 litres

$\Rightarrow 6x = 90 \Rightarrow x = 15$

$\therefore$ Water of pool Q = 15 litres

$\Rightarrow$ Water of pool P = 15 × 5

= 75 litres

So, quantity of water to be transferred from pool P to pool Q so that each pool contains 45 litres = 75 − 45 30 litres

Therefore, 30 litres of warer should be transferred.

5. (B) : Capacity of water pool

$= 49 \frac{5}{6}$ litres = $\frac{299}{6}$ litres

So, capacity of 3 such a pools

$= \frac{299}{6} \times 3$

$= \frac{299}{2}$ litres i.e. $149 \frac{1}{2}$ litres

6. (A) :

7. (B) : Length of wall painted green = 1.8 m

∴ Length of wall painted orange = 3 × 1.8 = 5.4 m

So, total Length of the wall = (1.8 + 5.4)m = 7.2 m

8. (B) : Length of crayon P
= (6.8 − 0.8)m = 6 m

Length of crayon Q
= (5.8 − 1.2)m = 4.6 m

∴ Required sum = (6 + 4.6) = 10.6 m

9. (C) : Temperature at 10 a.m = 32°C

Temperature at 11 a.m
= (32 + 7)°C = 39°C

Temperature at 1 p.m
= (39 − 6)°C = 33°C

10. (D) : Starting time = 8 . 38

Ending time = 10 . 19

∴ Required duration time = 1 hour 41 minutes

11. (D) : Cost of 1 watch at shop
$X = ₹ (\frac{1500}{2})$
$= ₹ 750$

Cost of 1 watch at shop Y =
$₹ (\frac{2100}{3})$
$= ₹ 700$

Cost of 1 watch at shop Z
= ₹ 600

12. (A) : Cost of two pairs of shoes at shop Y = ₹ 1700

Cost of 1 watch at shop Y
= ₹ 700

So, total amount spent by Mayur
= ₹ (1700 + 700) = ₹ 2400

13. (A) : Height of table = 1 m 14 cm = 1.14 m

∴ Height of chair = (1.14 ÷ 3)m
= 0.38 m

14. (B) : weight of 2 P = 16 kg

$⇒$ weight of 1 P = $\frac{16}{2}$ kg
= 8 kg

Also, weight P + weight of Q = 18 kg

$⇒$ 8 kg + weight of Q = 18 kg

$⇒$ weight of Q = 10 kg

15. (D) : According to question, we have

A = 6.8 × 4.2 = 28.56

And B (28.56 − 4)m = 24.56 m

16. (B) : Quantity of juice made by Kranti = 4.8 L

∴ Quantity of juice made by Mrunal = 3 × 3.8 = 14.4 L

So, total quantity of juice made by both of them together
= (4.8 + 14.4)L = 19.2 L

17. (A) : Let the total number of cupcakes be X.

∴ Number of egg cupcakes
$= \frac{1}{4}$ X

Number of stawberry cupcakes = $\frac{1}{8}$ X

And number of mango cupcakes $= X - (\frac{1}{4} X + \frac{1}{8} X)$

$= \frac{5}{8} X$

Now $\frac{1}{4} \times X \times 20 + \frac{1}{8} \times X \times 90 = 6.50 \times 10$ paise

$\Rightarrow \frac{40X + 90X}{8} = 650$

$\Rightarrow 130X = 5200 \Rightarrow X = 40$

$\therefore$ Number of mango cupcakes $= \frac{5}{8} \times 40 = 25$

So, money spent on mango cupcakes

$= (25 \times 5)$ paise $= 125$ paise

$= ₹ 1.25$

18. (C) : Total quantity of milk = 1 L 950 ml

$= 1.950$ L

Number of glasses = 5

$\therefore$ Quantity of milk in 1 glass

$= (1.950 \div 5)$ L $= 0.390$ ml

19. (C) : Capacity of coffee mug = 1 L 440

$= 1440$ ml

Capacity of 1 small coffee mug = 90 ml

So, number of people for whom coffee can be served

$= 1440 \div 90 = 16$

20. (C) : Total quantity of sweets Mayuri had = 480 kg

Quantity of sweets packed into container

$= \frac{3}{8} \times 480 = 180$ kg

$\therefore$ Quantity of sweets left = 480 – 180 = 300 kg

So, quantity of sweets to be packed in boxes

$= \frac{3}{5} \times 300 = 180$ kg

Number of boxes = 6

$\therefore$ Quantity of sweets in each boxe

$= 180 \div 6 = 30$ kg

21. (D) : Cost of 1 kg tomatos = ₹ 29.85

Cost of 3 kg tomatos =

₹ 29.85 × 3 = ₹ 89.55

Cost of 1 kg cucumbers = ₹ 38.80

Cost of 5 kg cucumbers = ₹ 38.80 × 5 = ₹ 194

So, total amount of money paid by Dipesh

$= ₹ 89.55 + ₹ 194 = ₹ 283.55$

22. (B) : Total length of the lace = 17.85m

Length of 1 small piece of lace = 0.35m

$\Rightarrow$ Length of 9 small pieces of lace

$= 9 \times 0.35 = 3.15$ m

$\therefore$ Length of the remaining piece of lace

$= (17.85 - 3.15)$ m 14.7 m

23. (A) : Total weight of mixture

$= (520 + 580)$g

$= 1100$ g

Number of packets = 5

weight of mixture in each packet

= (1100 + 5)g = 220 g

24. (C): Length of 1 small piece = $\frac{3}{4}$ m

∴ Length of 3 small pieces = $(\frac{3}{4} × 3)$ m $\frac{9}{4}$ m

Length of paper sheet left = $5\frac{3}{4}$ m = $\frac{23}{4}$ m

So, total length of the paper sheet

$= \frac{9}{4} + \frac{23}{4} = \frac{32}{4}$ = 8m

25. (A) : Distance travelled on Saturday = 125.20 km

Distance travelled on Sunday = 47.65 km

So, Swapnil drove (125.20 - 47.65) km

= 77.55 km less on Sunday than on Saturday

26. (A) : Quantity of lemonade made by Asha = 16.5 L

Quantity of lemonade made by Swapna = (3.5 + 16.5)L

$= 20$ L

Quantity of lemonade made by Swapna = $\frac{3}{4}$ × 20 = 15 L

∴ Quantity of rose lemonade left with Swapna = (20– 15)L

$= 5$ L

So, quantity of lemonade left with Asha = $\frac{5}{2}$ L = 2.5 L

∴ Quantity of lemonade sold

by Asha = (16.5 – 2.5)L = 14 L

27. (C) : Length of red garland = 2 m 98 cm = 2.98 cm

∴ Length of yellow garland = 2 × 2.98 m = 5.98m

Length of yellow garland used by Ankita = $1\frac{2}{5}$ m = 1.4 m

So, length of yellow garland left = (5.96 – 1.4) m = 4.56 m

Number of small of pieces cut = 4

∴ Length of each small piece = (4.56 ÷ 4)m = 1.14m

28. (D) : Weight of two P circle= 12 kg

∴ Weight of 1 circle P = $\frac{12}{2}$ = 6 kg

Now, Weight of circle P + Weight of circle Q = 14 kg

∴ Weight of circle Q = (14 – 6) kg = 8 kg

Also Weight of circle Q + Weight of circle R = 15 kg

⇒ Weight of circle R = (15 – 8) kg = 7 kg

29. (C) : Weight of (Ⓟ + Ⓢ + Ⓡ) = 540 g

Weight of (Ⓡ + Ⓢ) = 540 – weight of Ⓟ

.....(i)

⇒ Weight of (Ⓠ + Ⓡ + Ⓢ) = 600 g

$\Rightarrow$ Weight of (Q) + (540 - weight of (P)) = 600 (Using (i))

$\Rightarrow$ Weight of (Q) = 600 – 540 + weight of (P)

$\Rightarrow$ Weight of (Q) = 60 + weight of (P)

Also, weight of ((P) + (Q) + (Q)) = 660 g

$\Rightarrow$ Weight of ((P) + (60 + weight of (P)) + (60 + weight of (P)) = 660 g

$\Rightarrow$ Weight of 3 (P) + 120 g = 660 g

$\Rightarrow$ Weight of 3 (P) = 540 g

$\Rightarrow$ Weight of (P) = (540 + 3) g = 180 g

30. (B) : Weight of 🦆 = $1\frac{5}{6}$ kg = $\frac{11}{6}$ kg

Now $\frac{1}{12}$ kg + weight of 🟥 = $\frac{11}{6}$ kg

= Weight of 🟥 = $(\frac{11}{6} - \frac{1}{12})$ kg = $\frac{7}{4}$ kg

Now, $\frac{1}{8}$ kg + weight of 🟥 = Weight of 🦌

$\Rightarrow$ Weight of 🦌 = $(\frac{1}{8} + \frac{7}{4})$ kg = $\frac{15}{8}$ kg = $1\frac{7}{8}$ kg

1. (B) :

2. (B) :

3. (B) : 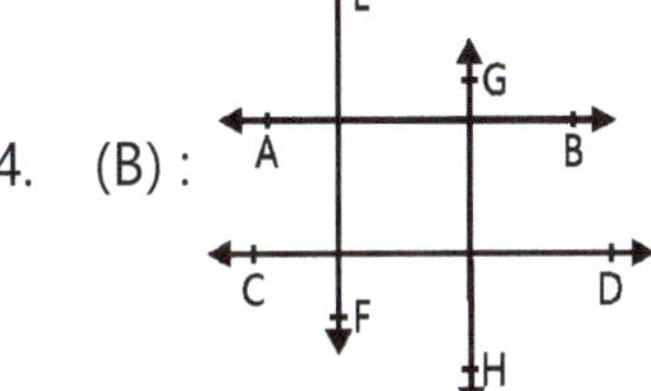

4. (B) :

Pairs of perpendicular lines are : (AB, EF); (CD, EF); (CD, GH): (AB, GH) i.e. 4 in number.

5. (A) :

6. (A) :

Here 4 pairs of acute angles are ; AIH, HGF, CDE and GHI

7. (D) :

8. (C) : Letter N, G, L and E have parallel lines.

9. (D) :

10. (B) :

11. (B) : Measure of angles in the figure = 180°

∴ Measure of angle drawn by Rohit = $\frac{1}{2} \times 180° = 90°$, which is the right angle

12. (B) : 

13. (B) :

14. (A) :

15. (B) : 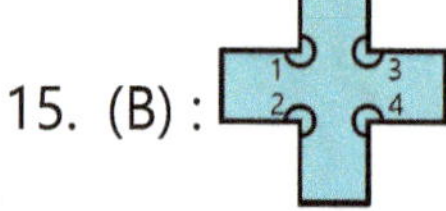

16. (B) :

17. (B) :

18. (D) :

19. (B) :

20. (B) :

21. (B) : 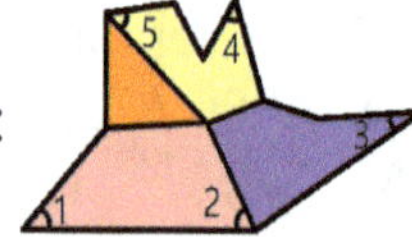

There are 5 acute angles in the given figure.

22. (C) :

23. (B) : 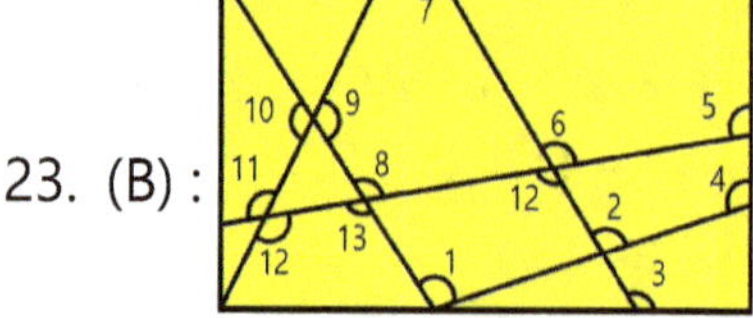

There are 13 angles which are more than 90° in the given figure.

24. (D) : The paires of intersecting lines are (AB, CD), (AB, GH), (GH, EF), (GH, CD)

25. (D) :

6. Perimeter and Area

1. (A) :

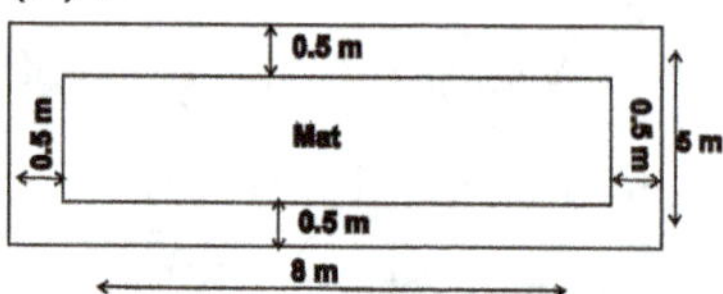

Lenght of the mat = [8 - (0.5 × 2)] m = (8 - 1) m = 7 m

Breadth of the mat = [5 - (0.5 × 2)] m = (5 - 1) m = 4 m

So, perimeterof the mat

= 2(Lenght + Breadth)

= 2(7 + 4)

= 2 × 11 = 22 m

2. (B) : Number of squares = 9

Now, 1 [ ] = 5 sq.unit

∴ Area of figure = 5 × 9 = 45 square units

3. (D) : After rearranging the given figure, we get the new figure as,

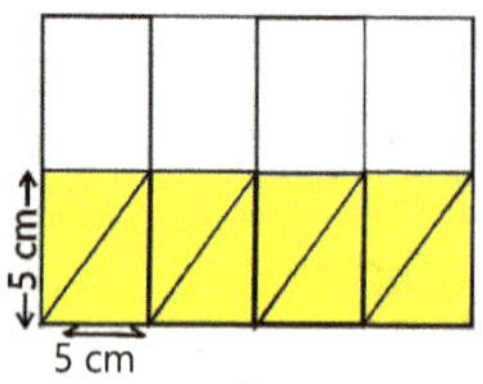

Area of 1 small rectangle

= 5 × 5 = 25 sq. cm

Number of shaded squares = 4

∴ Total shaded area

= (4 × 25) sq. cm = 100 sq. cm

4. (C) :

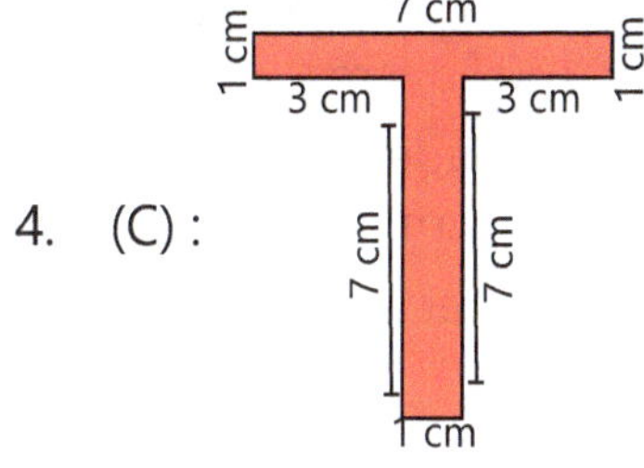

Perimeter of the figure = (7 + 1 + 7 + 3 + 1 + 7+ 1 + 3) cm = 30 cm

5. (A) : We have, PQ = 3 QR

$\Rightarrow$ PQ = 3 × 4 cm = 12 cm

PR = (12 + 4) cm = 16 cm

Also, RT = PR = 16 cm

$\therefore$ ST = 16 - 3 = 13 cm

So, perimeter of WPQSTU = (12 + 13 + 5 +12 + 13 + 5) cm = 60 cm

6. (C) : Area of small square = 2 × 2 = 4 sq. cm

Number of shaded squares = 22

$\therefore$ Shaded area = 22 × 4 = 88 sq. cm

7. (A) :

8. (C) : Length of TV screen = 60 cm

Perimeter of TV screen = 180 cm

$\therefore$ 2(Length + Breadth) = 180 cm

$\Rightarrow$ 2(60 cm length + Breadth) = 180 cm

$\Rightarrow$ 60 cm + Breadth = 90 cm

$\Rightarrow$ Breadth = (90 - 60)cm = 30 cm

9. (C) : Area of 1 small square = 3 × 3 = 9 sq. cm

number of shaded squares = 10

$\therefore$ Shaded area = 10 × 9 = 90 sq. cm

10. (C) : Perimeter of the given figure =(4 + 7 + 9 + 2 + 5 + 3 + 12 + 15 + 5 + 6 + 7 + 6 + 10 + 3 + 5 + 10)cm = 109 cm

11. (A) : Area of 1 ☐ = 3 sq.units

$\therefore$ Area of shape P = 14 × 3 = 42 sq. units.

Area of shape Q = 13 × 3 = 39 sq. units.

Area of shape R = 14 × 3 = 42 sq. units.

Area of shape S = 14 × 3 = 42 sq. units.

So, shape Q has the smallest area.

12. (D) : We have, PU = UT = TS = VS = VU = WV = PW

Now, PU + UT = 14 cm

$\Rightarrow$ PU + PV 14 cm $\Rightarrow$ PU = 7 cm

$\therefore$ Area of square PUVW = 7 × 7 = 49 sq. cm

Now, area of rectangle WQRS = 12 × 14 = 168 sq. cm

Area of $\triangle$ WQR = 168 ÷ 2 = 84 sq. cm

$\therefore$ Total shaded area = (49 + 84) = 133 sq. cm

13. (B) : Area of square ABCD = (15 × 15) sq. cm = 225 sq. cm

Area of square GEFC = (10 × 10) sq. cm = 100 sq. cm

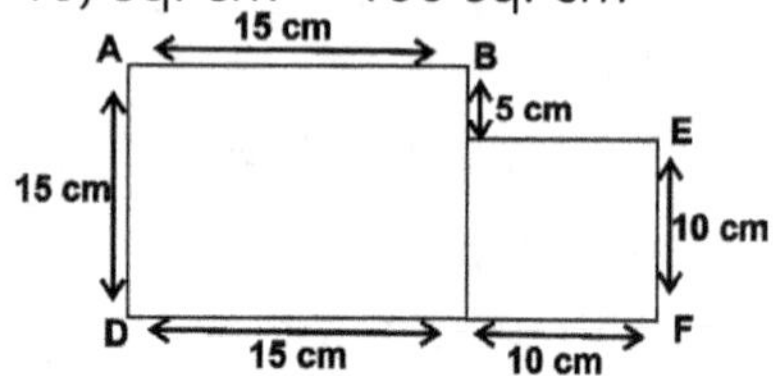

∴ Total area = (225 + 100) sq. cm = 325 sq. cm

14. (A) : Area of 1 small square = 2 × 2 = 4 sq. cm

Number of shaded squares = 16

∴ Area of shaded part = 16 × 4 = 64 sq. cm

15. (C) : Perimeter of the given figure = (1 + 8 + 4 + 8 + 6 + 5 + 4 + 3 +5 + 2 + 14) cm

= 60 cm

16. (B) : Perimeter of rectangle = 28 m

⇒ 2 (Length + breadth) = 28 m

⇒ 2(4 + 4 + breadth) = 28 m

⇒ Breadth = 6 m

Now, ST + TP = 6 m

⇒ 3m + TP = 6 m ⇒ TP = 3 m

∴ Perimeter of shaded figure

= TP +PQ + PV + VU + TU

= (3 + 8 + 3+ 5 + 5) m = 24 m

17. (D) : Area of square PQRS = 40 × 40 = 1600 sq. cm

Area of 1 rectangle = 10 × 8 = 80 sq. cm

So, area of 2 rectangles = 2 × 80 = 160 sq. cm

Hence, shaded area = (1600 - 160) sq. cm = 1440 sq. cm

18. (D) : Perimeter of each square = 32 cm

⇒ 4 × sides of square = 32 cm

⇒ Side of square = (32 + 4) cm = 8 cm

∴ Perimeter of the figure

= 18 × 8 = 112 cm

19. (B) : Area of larger square = (18 × 4) sq. cm = 72 sq. cm

Area of unshaded rectangle = (5 × 3) sq. cm = 15 sq. cm

Area of unshaded square

= (6 × 4) sq. cm = 24 sq. cm

∴ Area of shaded part

= 72 sq .cm - (15 + 24) sq. cm

= 39 sq. cm

20. (A) : Area of larger rectangle

=(35 × 20)sq. cm 700 sq .cm

Also, area of smaller rectangle = 587 sq. cm

∴ Area of shaded part = (700 - 587) sq. cm = 113 sq. cm

Now, Cost of colouring an area of 2 sq. cm = ₹ 70

∴ Cost of colouring an area of 1 sq. cm =₹ (70 ÷ 2) = ₹ 35

Hence cost of colouring the shaded area = ₹ (35 × 113)

= ₹ 3955

21. (C) : 1 ☐ = 1 sq. m

Area of the swimming pool = 35 × 1 = 35 sq. m

Area of the backyard = (11 × 6) sq. m = 66 sq. m

∴ Area of the backyard left for grass = (66 - 35)sq. m = 31 sq. m

22. (D) : Area of rectangular wall = 90 sq. m

Length × Breadth = 90 sq. m

⇒ 20 m × Breadth = 90 sq. m

⇒ Breadth = 18 m

∴ Perimeter = 2(Length + Breadth)

= 2(20 + 18) = 2 × 38 = 76 m

23. (D) : Length of rope required = 30 × 4 + 2 × 4 = 120 + 8 = 128 m

24. (A) : Total cost of fencing = ₹ 2100

Cost of fencing 1 m = ₹ 15

∴ Perimeter of field = 2100 ÷ 15 = 140m

⇒ 2(Length + Breadth) = 140 m

⇒ 2(Length + 20 m) = 140 m

⇒ Length + 20 m = 70 m

⇒ Length = (70 - 20) m = 50 m

25. (D) : Side of square garden = 50 m

So, perimeter of square garden = (59 × 4) m = 200 m

So, distance walk by lalit = 200 × 6 = 1200 m

26. (B) : Area of 1 small square = 2 × 2 = 4 sq. cm

Number of squares removed = 81 - 62 = 19

∴ Total area of squares removed = (19 × 4) sq. cm = 76 sq. cm

27. (C) : Unfolded form of the given tishu paper is show below.

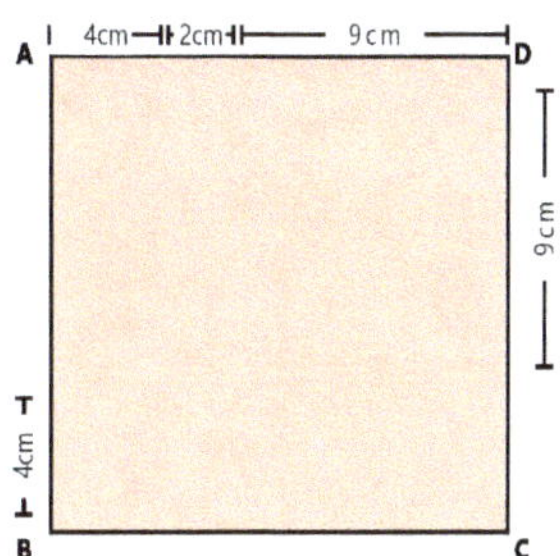

Area of tishu paper = AD × DC

= [(9 + 4) × (9 + 2 + 4)] sq. cm

= (13 × 15) sq .cm = 195 sq. cm

28. (C) : Area of figure = 90 sq. c,m

⇒ Area of 10 small squares = 90 sq.cm

⇒ Area of 1 small squares = (90 ÷ 10) sq. cm = 9 sq. cm

⇒ Side of 1 small square = 3 cm

∴ Perimeter of the figure (16 × 3) cm = 48 cm

29. (D) : Side of 1 square = 1 unit

Area of 1 square = (1 × 1) sq. unit = 1 sq. unit

(D) ; Area of 15 squares = 15 sq. unit

Perimeter = 2(5 + 3) = 16 units

30. **(C) :** Area of rectangle ABCJ = (20 × 10) sq. m = 200 sq. m

Area of recrangle JDEF = (18 × 8) sq. ,m = 144 sq. m

Area of rectangle IHGF = (2 × 6) sq. m = 12 sq. m

∴ Area of playground excluding tennis court

= Total area of the playground - Area of the tennis court

=(200 + 144 + 12 - 112) sq. m = 244 sq. m

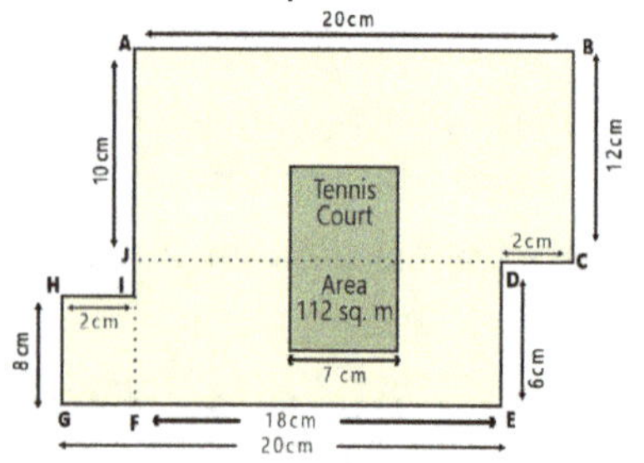

7. Symmetry

1. **(A):** 

So, 3 figure has line of symmetry

2. **(B) :** 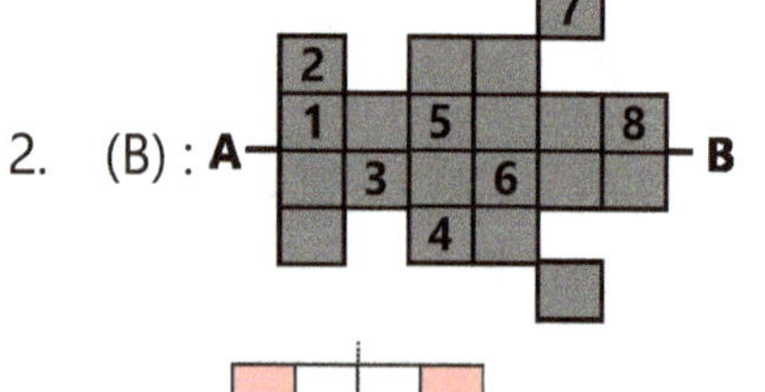

3. **(D) :**

4. **(D) :** 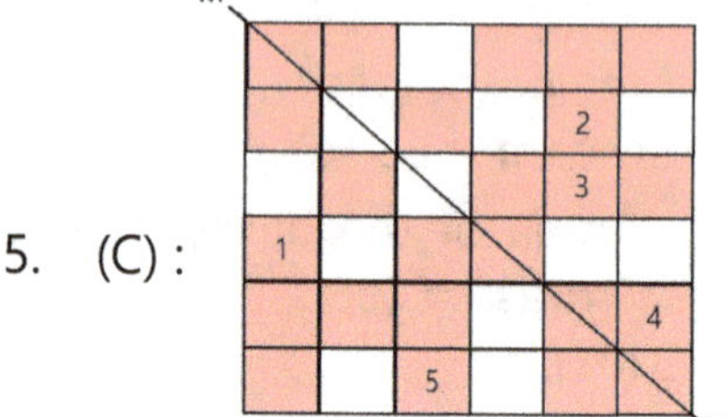

5. **(C) :**

6. **(D) :**

7. **(B) :**

8. **(D) :** 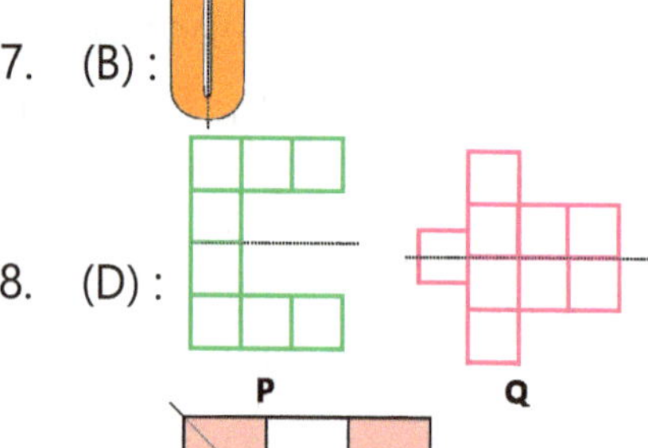

9. **(B) :**

10. **(A) :**

11. **(D) :** ALPHABETS

12. **(A) :**

13. **(B) :** 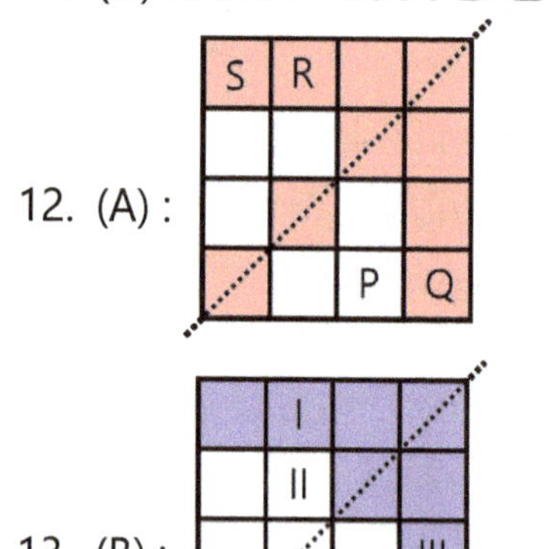

14. **(C) :**

15. (A) :

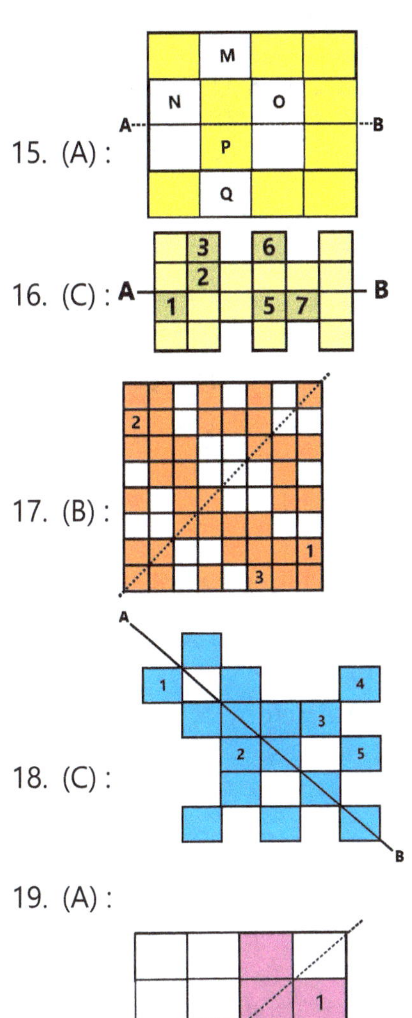

16. (C) :

17. (B) :

18. (C) :

19. (A) :

20. (A) :

8. Data Handling

1. (A) :

2. (B) : Number of students who like basketball = 20

Number of student who like badminton = 15

∴ Total number of students who like basketball and badminton together

= 20 + 15

3 (C) : Number of student who like jogging = 20

Number of student who like cycling = 10

∴ Number of students who like jogging than cycling

= 20 – 10 = 10

4. (C) : Number of students who participated in music

= 17 × 5 = 85

5. (D) : Number of students who participated in dancing

= 17 × 8 = 136

6. (A) : Number of students who participated in singing

= 17 × 3 = 51

Number of students who participated in painting

= 17 × 3 = 51

So, total number of students who participated in singing and painting together

= 51 + 51 = 102

Now, number of students who participated in art & craft = 17 × 9 = 153

∴ Required difference

= 153 – 102 = 51

7. (D) : Number of bikes sold in first 3 weeks = 2 + 4 + 3 = 9

Number of bikes sold in first 2 weeks = 6 + 9 = 15

∴ Difference between the number of bikes sold

= 15 – 9 = 6

8. (C) : Total number of bikes sold in first 5 weeks

= 2 + 4 + 3 + 6 + 9 = 24

Amount made by selling in 1 bike = ₹ 20000

∴ Total amount = ₹ (20000 × 24) = ₹ 480000

9. (B) : Number of students who choose history = 4 × 4 = 16

Number of students who choose hindi = 4 × 3 = 12

∴ Required difference

= 16 – 12 = 4

10. (B) :

11. (D) : Total numbers of students = 20 + 16 + 8 + 20 + 12 = 76

12. (B) : Number of pizzas sold on Thursday = 30

Number of pizzas sold on Monday = 50

∴ Required difference

= 50 – 30 = 20

13. (A) : Greatest numbers of pizzas sold = 55

Least number of pizzas sold = 30

∴ Required difference

= 55 – 30 = 25

14. (C) : Number of pizzas sold on Tuesday = 40

Profit made on each pizzas

= ₹ 15

∴ Total profit made

= ₹ (15 × 40) = ₹ 800

15. (B) :

16. (A) : Number of residents at Bandra = 6000

Number of residents at Parel = 4400

∴ Required difference

= 6000 – 4400 = 1600

17. (D) : Total numbers of residents

= 3500 + 4100 + 4400 + 3400 + 6000 + 6000

= 27400

18. (B) :

19. (A) : Height of Sayali = 150 cm

Height of Prakash = 100 cm

∴ Required difference

= (150 – 100) cm

= 50 cm

20. (D) :

21. (C) : Total amount of milk used = 20 + 15 + 30 + 40 + 35 = 140L

Amount of milk used in August = 40 L

∴ Required fraction $= \dfrac{40}{140} = \dfrac{2}{7}$

22. (B) : Weight of an empty container = 80 g

Weight of ball P + weight of container = 180 g

$\Rightarrow$ Weight of ball P=(180 – 80)g = 100 g

Weight of (ball P + ball B + container) = 360 g

$\Rightarrow$ Weight of ball Q = (36 – 180)g = 180 g

Weight of (ball P + ball Q + ball R + container) = 500 g

$\Rightarrow$ Weight of ball R= (600 – 360) g = 140 g

Now, weight of (ball P+ ball Q + ball R + ball S + container) = 580 g

$\Rightarrow$ Weight of ball S = (580 – 500) g = 80 g

So, ball Q is the heaviest.

23. (B) : Total amount of money saved by Gayatri

= ₹ (40 + 60 + 70 + 100 + 110) =₹ 380

Total amount of money saved by Anjali

= ₹ (60 + 30 + 90 + 90 + 120) =₹ 390

So, Anjali saved (₹ 390 - ₹ 380) = ₹ 10 more than Gayatri.

24. (A) : Total amount of money donated = ₹ 1995

Amount of money donated by each people = ₹ 19

Let the number of peoples of place D who donated money be x.

According to question, we have

$(20 + 30 + 25 + x + 15) \times 19$ = 1995

$\Rightarrow 90 + x = 105 \Rightarrow x = 15$

So, required numbers of peoples = 15

25. (D) : Total amount earned by selling cabbages = ₹ 300

Cost of 12 cabbages = ₹ 6

So, cost of 1 cabbage =₹ $\dfrac{6}{12}$

=$(\dfrac{1}{2})$

$\therefore$ Required number of cabbages

= $300 + \dfrac{1}{2}$ = 600

9 Logical Resoning

1. (B) : According to question, we have

9 students
Nitu
4 students
Sonali
5 students

So, number of students in the line = 9 + 1 + 4 + 1 + 5 = 20

2. (C) : The Pattern followed is:

$4 \xrightarrow{+6} 10 \xrightarrow{+6} 16 \xrightarrow{+6} 22 \xrightarrow{+6} 28$

$C \xrightarrow{+2} E \xrightarrow{+2} G \xrightarrow{+2} I \xrightarrow{+2} K$

3. (C) :

Mirror

4. (A) : The order from the eldest to the youngest is

Madhav, Neeraj / Rohan, Rohan / Neeraj, Dinesh

So, Madhav is the eldest.

5. (C) : 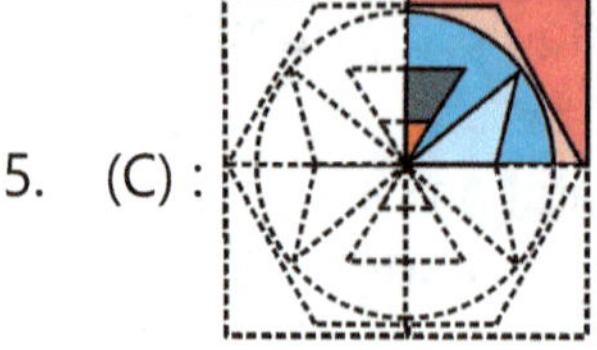

6. (C) :

Pranav Mahesh Kabir Girish Raj

∴ Girish is secound from the right end.

7. (B) : 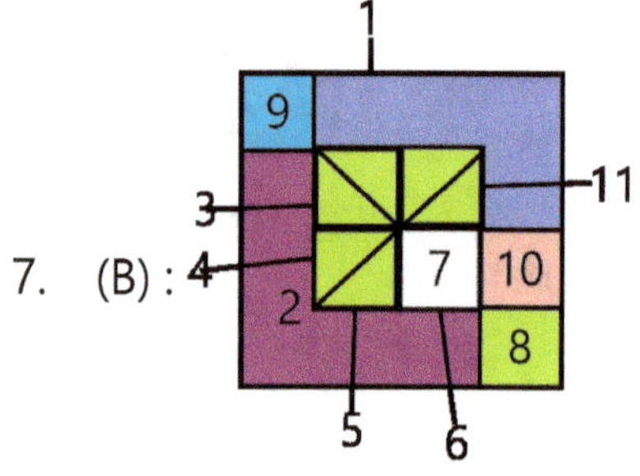

8. (C) : The left element and the right element interchange their position, the shaded part of the element become unshaded and vice-versa. Also, the element which is at downward position goes upward.

9. (A) : MANGO — Water Layer

10. (B) :

11. (A) : Total number of boxes =
2 + 4 + 6 + 8 + 10 = 30

12. (A) : Total possible combinations = 4 × 5 = 20

13. (B) : The correct order is Village, City, State, Country, World i.e : 4, 1, 5, 3, 2

14. (C) : 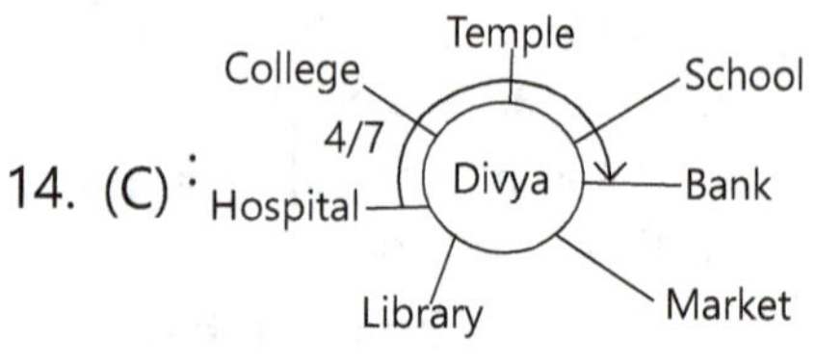

So, Divya will facing the Bank

15. (D) : The rule followed is,
(4 × 9) - (5 × 2) = 36 - 10 = 26
(3 × 8) - (11 × 4) = 44 - 24 = 20
So, (12 × 4) - (7 × 3) = 48 - 21 = 27

16. (A) : Pattern repeats itself after every 4 figure

17. (B) : The rule followed is,
(5 × 4) × 3 = 60
and (3 × 8) × 3 = 72
Similarly (2 × 7) × 3 = 42

18. (A) :

19. (B) : the new arrangement of letter is, ATPULPOION
So, nineth letter from the right end is T.

20. (D) :

21. (A) :

22. (A) : 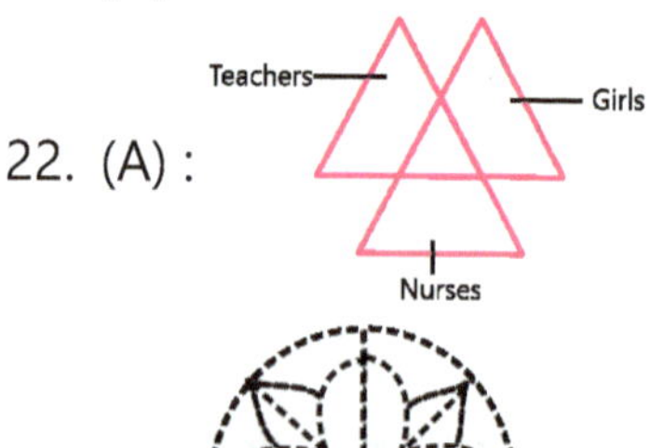

23. (C) : 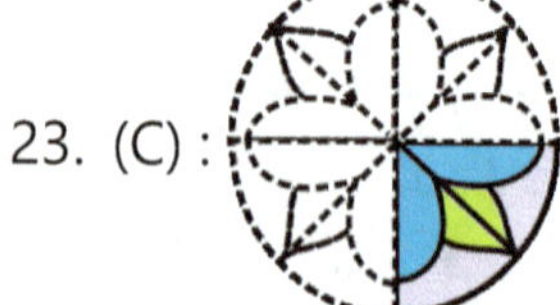

24. (A) : 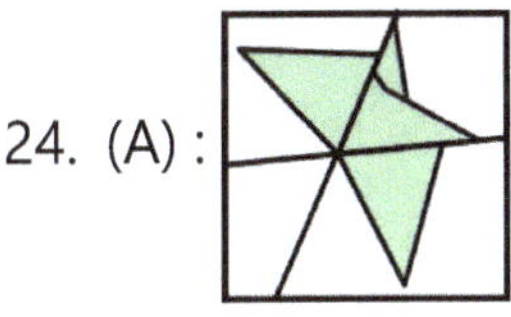

25. (D) : We have,

N → O, O → P, R → S, M → N, A → B, L → I (each +1)

Similarly,

D → E, I → J, F → G, F → G, I → J, C → D, U → V, L → M, T → U (each +1)

26. (B) : 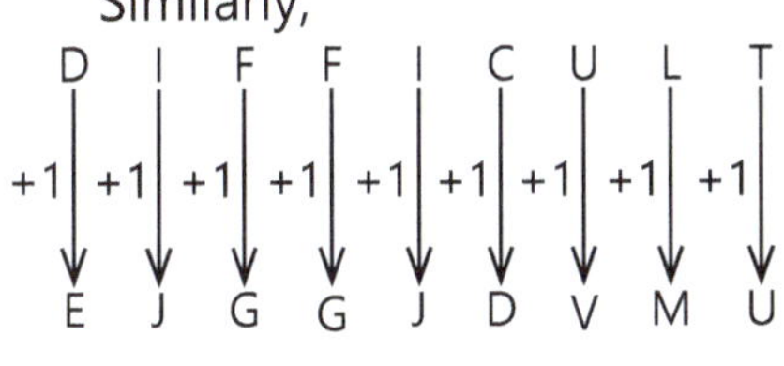

27. (B) : Third Sunday of May 20XX falls on 18 th May. And, fourth day after 18 th May is 22 May.

28. (C):  _ _ _ _ _ _ _ _ _ _ – Water layer

29. (B) : Number 2 is common i triangle, circle, square only. So number 2 indicates girls who are actor and model.

30. (D) : Water is used to drink when one is thirsty, but 'water' is called 'light'.